BUILDING SUCCESS

Bill Osher, Ph.D.

Joann Ward, Ed.S.

KENDALL/HUNT PUBLISHING COMPANY
4050 Westmark Drive   Dubuque, Iowa 52002

THE COVER DESIGN

The act of *Building Success* can take on a variety of different interpretations.

Building suggests the creation of something. Building is an active, ongoing process. Planning, initiative, seizing opportunities, and getting experience are the building blocks for success. Combined with the development of the skill set found in this text, they can become the foundation for any goal. The momentum of building is in the upward direction, with no limit in sight. The viewpoint on the cover illustration suggests that you, the reader, are looking up at a sky of endless possibilities.

Success means realizing your aspirations. It encompasses not only academics, but also personal and professional goals. Success itself is not a learned skill, but you can learn the skills that will enable you to build success. Take this chance to learn and refine these skills, as they will be helpful throughout your life.

As with any task, it is best not to struggle by yourself. Teamwork and collaboration can bring results unattainable by one person alone. I encourage you to seek opportunities to work together with your peers throughout your college career.

~ Erica Young
Industrial Design 2001

CONTENTS

CHAPTER 1
Building Success

How to Succeed

Every year about three million students start college. Only half of them will ever graduate. Of those who do get their diplomas, approximately fifty percent do so with only the haziest of career goals and no real job in sight. Among those who graduate employable, a still smaller percentage enters the job market poised for success. They are not only employable, but they will start work in fields they enjoy with opportunities for advancement. We wrote this book to tell you how to become one of those success stories.

This book tells you how to succeed in college and how to use college to ensure professional success. We even have some things to say about how to succeed in life. There is a lot of literature on success. Much of it is overblown psychobabble: "If you can dream it, you can do it." While dreams do play a role in success, dreaming of wealth and fame by no means guarantees that you will ever have them. There is, however, some very solid research on how to succeed. Scholars have studied successful people and know pretty well what attitudes and habits led to their success. These same attitudes will also get you to where you want to go. In fact, we have conducted research ourselves on what enables students to succeed. Whether you want to succeed in college, in a career, or in life, we can tell you what it will take.

When we ask students what it takes to succeed in school, their first answer is often "intelligence." The smarter a person is, the better they'll do in school. This is not true. While a certain minimal amount of intelligence is required to succeed in college, there are other factors that play a huge role in a student's performance. You've probably known bright people who are less successful than the average person. And you've probably known people of average intelligence who are highly successful because of key attitudes and habits. Naturally, it's nice when you are highly intelligent AND possess the key traits and habits. Then your prospects are especially bright. Unfortunately, you can't change your intelligence. Fortunately, you can change your attitude and habits—what you might call your character. There is a "character of success." It is comprised of three simple elements: thinking like a successful person, acting like a successful person, and persisting like a successful person.

■ The Character of Success

Successful Thinking: THE MOTIVE TO ACHIEVE. The most successful people have achievement on the brain. They are preoccupied with competing effectively, reaching goals, overcoming obstacles, and using resources. Whether in the classroom, the sports arena, or the business world, high achievers are thinking about better ways to reach their goals.

Successful Action: COMMITMENT. Not only must you think about success, you must actually take those steps that create success. Wanting success is a necessary first step. Behaving successfully must come next. You must be committed. In college, that means studying regularly and using effective learning techniques. It is one thing to talk the talk. Quite another to walk the walk. Commitment, then, is doing those things required of you to succeed academically and professionally.

Successful Persistence: RESILIENCE. You must be tough. It is not enough to get started. It is not enough even to keep going for a while. You must persist in the face of obstacles, setbacks, barriers, and defeats. A recruiter for a large corporation once told me that he always asks candidates about their experiences with failure and defeat. If they've had none, he will not hire them. He can't be sure that they won't bail out when the going gets tough. Unless a person is willing to persist in the face of failure, a person's ability to succeed is profoundly impaired.

Success, then, is built on Achievement, Commitment, and Resilience. You must be motivated. You must turn your motivation into action. And you must persist when the going gets tough. We've already said that character is something you can cultivate. You can build Achievement, Commitment, and Resilience. If you are serious about success and are willing to put in the effort in the right way, it is virtually inevitable that you will succeed!

Other Success Factors

Understanding your environment. Another piece of information you need in order to succeed—you must know the domain in which you wish to succeed. That means you need to know the college environment. We have six degrees between us, and we've worked on college campuses for many years. We know how to "work the system." You need to know it too. While you are immersed in college life, bear in mind that you're preparing for life "in the real world." You should also have some knowledge of that world. It is particularly important for you to know something about the world of work you'll be entering in the early 21st Century.

Influencing others. While striving individually to reach worthwhile goals is crucial to success, it is difficult in college or in life to succeed in isolation. A large part of success comes from one's ability to work with and through others. School, work, and life are all a lot easier when you have learning partners to stimulate your thinking, colleagues who respect you enough to listen to your input, and friends to support you. In fact, most important goals in life require leadership—your ability to motivate others to work willingly for a common cause.

Understanding your goals. *The American Heritage Dictionary* defines success as "the achievement of something desired, planned, or attempted." In other words, in order to succeed you must reach a goal. Before you can attain a goal, however, you must know what that goal is. Before you can succeed in college, then, you must have goals. You need a reason for being here.

There are lots of reasons why people attend college. Some go because they didn't know what else to do. Their friends were going. Their parents expected them to enroll. Hey, it beats working! With no clearer purpose than any of these, your chances of getting your money's worth from college are not good. And college is an expensive proposition—over a hundred thousand dollars for a top private school, as much as fifty thousand for some state schools.

If you've started college without a clear mission, that can be remedied. You can resolve to create one for yourself. There are, of course, some lofty reasons—to become an educated person, learn more about yourself and the world, and develop a meaningful philosophy of life. Chances are good, however, that your top reasons for going to college are to get a good job that pays well. Research conducted by Alexander Astin of the University of California at Los Angeles has repeatedly found career advancement and financial security to be the top reasons students have gone to school for the past several years.

We have some good news for you . . . and some bad. The good news is that college degrees can make a huge difference in your career opportunities and your earning power. (See the bar graph in this chapter on Household Income and Educational Attainment.) This is probably something you already more or less knew. The bad news is that a college degree, in and of itself, guarantees nothing. Bill Gates, the Microsoft Czar and the richest man in the world, is a college dropout. There are PhD's who drive cabs and wait tables. College, like life, is an opportunity. It is, in fact, one of the biggest opportunities you'll ever have. An opportunity, however, is just that. Unless you take advantage of the opportunities college provides, you could be wasting a lot of time and money.

Another thing to take into consideration is that "career success" and "wealth" are not really goals. They are too abstract and general. You might find it helpful to think of the "goal line" in football or the net in hockey or the rim in basketball. Each of these goals is concrete, and visible. They are targets, and players and spectators alike know whether they have been hit. We think it is useful to think of goals as targets such as those comprised of concentric circles with a bull's eye in the center. You succeed in archery, darts, or riflery by aiming carefully, shooting accurately and hitting the center of the target. It's pretty much the same in college and in careers. Without goals, you can't very well succeed. Put another way, if you don't know where you're headed, any road will do, but you probably won't like where you wind up!

SMART Goals. In this book, we suggest you employ a system for setting goals. We did not invent this system, and there are other systems that work. We encourage you, however, to set goals that are:

> **S**pecific
> **M**easureable
> **A**ction oriented
> **R**ealistic
> **T**imely

We'll tell you more about how to set goals and reach them throughout this text. We specifically elaborate on the SMART system in Chapter 3. At this point, we want to say that the "other success factors" cited above—understanding your environment, influencing others, and understanding your goals—are also factors over which you have some control. You can learn the rules that govern the college environment. (See Chapter 4.) You can become informed about the 21st Century. (See section in this chapter below.) You can develop your people skills. (See Chapters 13 and 14 on Teamwork and Leadership.) You can clarify your own career path and set goals which will move you along it. (See Chapter 5 on Career Planning.)

■ Succeeding in the 21st Century

The forces that will dominate the 21st Century have been in operation before the year 2000 appeared on the calendar. The computer has been king for over a decade. Many of the commercials run during Superbowl XXXIV promoted .Com products and organizations. The leading headlines for several days in February of 2000 have concerned hackers flooding important Internet sites. We are already in the Information Age. If you ignore the challenges it poses and wander casually into the future, you could be a casualty.

■ The Information Age

We've argued that in addition to core character traits, success depends upon understanding the situation in which you find yourself. You must understand your collegiate environment (Chapter 4) and you must have some understanding of the forces at work in the world today. What are the implications of living in the Information Age?

You may already have heard of futurist Alvin Toffler. His best selling books include *Future Shock* and *The Third Wave*. He and John Naisbitt (who wrote *Megatrends*) are probably the two most widely read futurists who write for the general public. Toffler argues that civilization can be divided into three epochs: agricultural, industrial, and informational. (Toffler follows Daniel Bell's three ages—preindustrial, industrial, and postindustrial—which were posited in *The Coming of Post-Industrial Society*.)

The Agricultural Age

Toffler states that up until about 8,000 years ago, humans lived a tribal, nomadic existence. Our hunter-gatherer ancestors were perennially on the move, following the animals which provided the food. As humans began to farm instead of forage and herd instead of hunt, a radically different society evolved. Farming required permanent settlements so crops could be tended. Settlements grew into cities, and society became more diverse and complex. While there were warriors and priests, artists

and craftspeople, kings and scholars, most humans worked the soil. The question, "What will you be when you grow up?" would have puzzled most people. They would spend their lives struggling to survive by planting crops and harvesting them. The history of civilization has been predominantly agrarian.

The Industrial Age

The agricultural age began to decline in the 17th Century when people began to make products in much greater quantities. Eventually, the power of steam was harnessed which led to factories capable of mass production. As the Industrial Revolution spread throughout most of the globe, the way in which fundamental societal institutions were organized changed. The change was often painful. Human muscle could not compete with steam power and gears, and many workers lost their jobs. John Henry, the steel driving man, lost his life, the ballad says, because he couldn't keep up with a machine. Eventually, most men toiled in factories or in the mines which provided the fuel to power the factories. Mass production permitted the accumulation of much greater wealth.

The Information Age

In 1955, white-collar workers surpassed the number of blue-collar workers in the United States. For the first time in history, more people earned their money pushing pencils behind a desk than pushing parts on an assembly line. The significance of this is the pencil pusher manipulates information instead of machinery. Since 1955, the number of information workers has grown; the number of machine operators has declined. Increasingly, the Information Age is built upon the computer. It permits the power harnessed in the Industrial Age to be wielded much more effectively and productively.

From plow to machine to computer. From farm to factory to office. From farmer to machinist to expert. Work is changing. Government, families, and communities are changing. Society is changing as we rush further into an Information Age already begun. We believe there are several features that characterize the Informa-

tion Age. These principles already permeate every aspect of contemporary life. Their power and influence will only increase. Ignore them at your peril!

Key Principles of the Information Age

■ **Change will be pervasive and rapid.** Technological innovation alters civilization, and civilization impacts our lives. This has always been true, but change occurs more rapidly today than in the past. The agricultural age evolved over thousands of years. The industrial age matured over hundreds. The information age has exploded within decades. The invention of the printing press laid the foundation for near-universal literacy in the developed world. The education of the masses became a reality, however, only after some hundreds of years. The computer and advanced telecommunications laid the foundation for a global economy. That reality has emerged in the last thirty years. Nations, industries, and companies rise and fall. Those who best cope with constant change will endure and prosper. Joel Baker in *Future Edge* recounts the following true story of the challenges and opportunities associated with change. In 1968, Switzerland dominated the watchmaking industry worldwide. They made the best watches. They worked unceasingly to improve them. It was understandable then that they would garner 80% to 90% of the industry's profits worldwide. Yet, by 1980, the Swiss' profit share had dropped to less than 20%. Why? Because they did not adjust rapidly enough to change.

What happened? The Japanese adopted and developed the electronic quartz movement, and that became the benchmark of the watchmaking industry. What makes this story so ironic is that it was the Swiss themselves who invented the technology. Their corporate leaders, however, did not anticipate the changing demands of their customers and so rejected this technological innovation. Japan now leads the world in the sale of time pieces.

Adjusting to the differences between high school and college life has always been a challenge. The changes today are, however, more profound and far-reaching. You'll rely heavily on campus computing to succeed. You'll access your syllabi via course Web sites. You'll get announcements via listserves and newsgroups. You'll collaborate via e-mail. There will be more diversity among your classmates and probably among the faculty as well. As the world changes, so does the curriculum. Deans and professors hotly debate which books are crucial for you to read and which topics are essential for you to master.

It's not just that change is pervasive in the information age; it's also that change occurs rapidly. If anything characterizes contemporary society, it is speed. Time is already money in the business world. Meeting deadlines, working overtime, doing business in a "New York minute"—these are common practices today. Federal Express was built on the need of businesses to deliver fast. This trend will only increase in the 21st Century. Letters used to take months. Now they take only a few days, but that's still not fast enough. That's why people now use e-mail instead of "snail mail." The phone and the FAX carry information at the speed of light. One way to represent the speed that characterizes contemporary life is through the speed with which computer chips process information. The October 1995 *National Geographic* devoted an entire article to the Information Revolution. That, in itself is revealing: cyberspace has become the geography of our time. Among the observations made was the breathtakingly rapid increasing speed of computers: In 1971, a chip could perform 60,000 "additions" per second; in 1974, 290,000; in 1979, 330,000; in 1982, 900,000; in 1985, 5,500,000; in 1989, 20,000,000; in 1993, 100,000,000; in 1995, 250,000,000 "additions" per second. In twenty-five years, the speed of computers has increased four thousand-fold!

In 1965, Gordon Moore, co-founder of Intel Corporation, predicted that computing power would double every 18 months. "Moore's Law," as it has come to be known, has proven to be uncannily accurate in forecasting the rapid increase in the speed with which computers work. While doubling in power approximately every year and a half, might not seem impressive, it is. Since the 1950's until 1997, computing speed has increased by a factor of *ten billion.* By the time you read this, it will have grown even faster!

As smaller chips are manufactured with more circuits, computers get faster and smaller. As computers become faster and smaller, they become more portable and more affordable. As portability and affordability increases, so does the speed with which business and industry is conducted. While the computer is central to the speed that characterizes the Information Age, telecommunications is also a factor. Increasingly, you can do business with anybody, anywhere, anytime by phone. Moreover, all industrialized countries are competing with each other in a global economy. One way the competition is waged is by speed. Getting products and services to customers quickly is a key to success in today's business world. We are traveling in the 21st Century with the foot of society firmly pressing the accelerator to the floorboard.

■ **Knowledge is power.** Ed Cornish, in the January/February 1996 edition of *The Futurist*, predicts that education may become compulsory for adults as well as young people. Technological change causes ripples throughout society. Life-long learning will be essential to keep up with those ripples.

In the Information Age, strength and power are related to knowledge. The strongest countries are those with the best educational systems who produce the best scientists, technicians, and managers. Japan, for example, is a small, crowded island nation with relatively few natural resources. Yet, its economy is the second largest in the world. Why? Because its educational system produces technically skilled citizens with very few falling through the cracks. At this writing, Japan is suffering from an economic recession due to problems in its banking system, but no one expects Japan to be anything other than a major economic force for the foreseeable future.

When compared with Japan, the United States high school dropout and illiteracy rates make it very difficult for us to compete industrially as a nation. True, we remain the largest economy in the world, but our position is much more vulnerable than it was 50 years ago. Our school children consistently score less well on standardized tests than do most other developed nations.

As with nations, the strongest corporations are those which attract and cultivate intellectual talent and know how to nurture its expression. Currently, it is considered vital for any business enterprise to be "a learning organization."

And finally, for individuals in the Information Age, the height of one's career ladder will be largely determined by the depth and breadth of one's knowledge. College is probably the best chance you'll ever have to strengthen and lengthen that ladder.

The implications of this truth are far-reaching. If you want to prosper in the 21st Century, you must do it with your brain. That means attending college and getting one or more degrees is more important than it has ever been. The 1992 U.S. Census reports the following correlation between education and income:

Educational Attainment	*Household Income*
Less than 9th Grade	$13,300
9th to 12th Grade	$17,300
High School Degree	$29,000
Attended College	$35,300

College Degree	$49,500
Master's Degree	$57,900
Doctorate	$70,100
Professional Degree	$84,900

Education has been related to success for many years. Its significance today is even more profound. The new census will surely reveal an even greater disparity between educational haves and have-nots. Russell Jacoby observes in *Dogmatic Wisdom, How the Culture Wars Divert Education and Distract America*, that in the 1970's white college graduates earned only 18% more than white male high school graduates. By 1989, the difference had shot up to 45%. For women and blacks the difference is even more striking. By 1989 the white women college graduates earned 75% more than their high school graduate counterparts. In that same year, African American female college graduates made 92% more than their high school graduate peers.

Of course, education is about much more than getting a string of degrees. What really counts is learning how to learn and becoming a continuous learner throughout your life so that you can keep us with change.

Derek Price charts in *Little Science, Big Science* the phenomenal accelerating growth of scientific knowledge in the last few hundred years. In the middle of the 17th Century there were two scientific journals. One hundred years later there were ten. Fifty years after that there were 100. Fifty years after that, 1,000. By 1963, there were approximately 50,000! By the time you read this, there will probably over 100,000 scientific journals regularly published. This means that scientific knowledge doubles every few years. Petersen, in *The Road to 2015*, guestimates it doubles every 18 months. It's extremely difficult to keep up with all the advances in any one field. It's impossible to keep up with the advances in all fields. There's even a term for this state of affairs. It's called information overload.

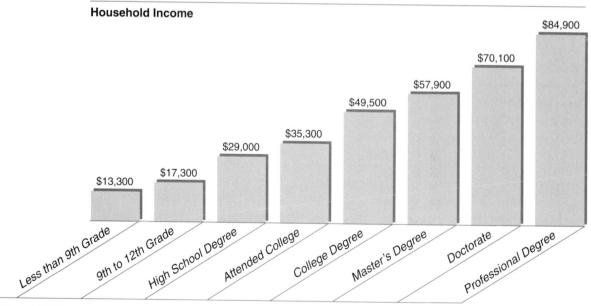

Household Income

$13,300 — Less than 9th Grade
$17,300 — 9th to 12th Grade
$29,000 — High School Degree
$35,300 — Attended College
$49,500 — College Degree
$57,900 — Master's Degree
$70,100 — Doctorate
$84,900 — Professional Degree

Educational Attainment

Petersen further observes that a person who reads an entire copy of the Sunday *New York Times* would take in more information in one afternoon than the average citizen in Thomas Jefferson's day would within a lifetime. There are many implications to the problem posed by information overload. Which information do we regard as essential to pass on to the next generation? What core knowledge must college students master? How can you as a citizen stay informed? How can you as a professional keep abreast of your field? And how do you winnow out the useful, reliable information from all the garbage that's on the internet?

■ **Diversity dominates.** We live in a global economy, buying, selling, and trading with every part of the world. The planet will continue to shrink as transportation grows faster and instantaneous communication networks reach all areas of the globe. It is highly likely that you will work outside of the continental United States at some point during your career. You will be called upon to do business with people whose culture, language, and beliefs differ from yours. The composition of the American workforce is also growing more diverse. By the year 2000, the percentage of white non-Hispanic men, historically the largest segment comprising our labor force, will have shrunk, while the percentage of African-American, Asian, and Hispanic job holders will have risen. Women of all races will account for almost half of the labor force in the U.S. Your colleagues will be of African, Hispanic, European, and Asian origins, as well as mixtures thereof. Historically, career women could choose between nursing and teaching. Today, women are entering science and engineering, law and medicine, management and the executive suite. You will work for and with women.

The World Village Project captures the flavor of the future by creating an imaginary village of 1,000 people to represent the **demographics** of the entire planet. In this village, there would be:

- 584 Asians
- 28 East Europeans
- 67 West Europeans
- 55 Former Soviet citizens
- 124 Africans
- 84 Latin Americans
- 52 North Americans
- 6 Australia/New Zealand

There would be:
- 327 Christians
- 178 Muslims
- 132 Hindus
- 62 Buddhists
- 45 Atheists
- 3 Jews
- 86 Other
- 167 Non-Religious

While the planet as a whole has always been characterized by racial, cultural, and ethnic diversity, this variety has a much greater impact upon us today because telecommunications and transportation have eroded most of the national and geographical barriers that historically have separated us. I (Bill) live in Atlanta, Georgia, a scant few years ago the heart of the deep South. When I finish this chapter I will drive to The Dekalb International Farmers Market which serves a thoroughly international customer base and is staffed by employees from every continent. Each wears a name tag indicating the various languages that individual speaks. I can buy collard greens, pork chops, and catfish. I can also buy squid, jicama, and lemon grass. This Farmers Market is a snapshot of the future demographics of the United States.

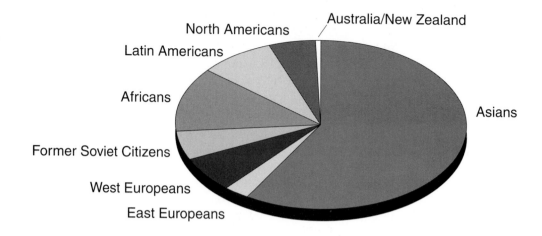

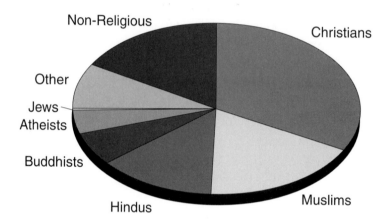

Because residential/public schooling patterns tend to remain ethnically more homogeneous, you may not have had much experience with diversity. Chances are your collegiate experience has already revealed a much richer diversity—racially, ethnically, nationally, religiously, and politically than what you were used to. While the differences among your classmates may be new, they suggest the way things will be. Notice also the different backgrounds of the faculty. In particular, you may find the science and engineering professors to have countries of origin outside the United States.

■ **The secure, lifetime job is a thing of the past.** The prevalence of change will have a big impact on your career. Employees no longer work for a giant corporation over a thirty year career that culminates in a retirement dinner and a gold watch. People increasingly have many jobs and a number of careers. Some would say that the traditional job is an endangered species. Downsizing has become a way of life in the corporate world, affecting blue-collar and white collar employees alike. More and more people will manage their own careers, selling their expertise to a variety of individuals and organizations as self-employed entrepreneurs.

If you end up working for many companies instead of one or two, there are a number of important implications. How will you find the many jobs or projects which you must piece together into a career? With no pension, how will you ensure your long term financial security? Who will your colleagues be?

■ **Enormous challenges loom ahead.** As the world population grows on a planet that doesn't, there are numerous obstacles to peace and prosperity looming on the horizon: overpopulation, environmental degradation, violence, disease, and poverty. Any one of these issues could fill a book if not an entire library, but that is beyond the scope of this text.

While the need to address such profound societal problems is great, it would appear that the will to do so is lacking. The American political system often seems to be embroiled in partisan bickering that leads to inaction. The American electorate is not well informed: many voters don't know who their own congressman/woman is. A surprising number of eligible citizens are not registered to vote, and many who are registered don't actually participate in elections. If you're persuaded that the solutions must come from outside the different levels of government, the news is not necessarily any more encouraging. Charitable contributions have declined in recent years, and people are less likely to volunteer their time to civic organizations. According to the 1999 Cooperative Institutional Research Project, the interest of college freshmen in community service has continued to decline.

So there it is. You face a strikingly different world than your parents faced when they were your age. Can you keep up with rapidly changing technology? Will you flounder in an ocean of information? What will the world of work be like? How will you manage your career? Will public schools be good enough to educate your children? Will your confidence in our government and its elected officials continue to plummet? Will your streets and neighborhoods be safe? Will you want to live behind walled and gated communities? Change is often frightening and painful. It ushers in tremendous challenges, but it can also offer unprecedented opportunities. Will you be prepared to meet the challenges and seize the opportunities?

■ Implications and Applications

The purpose of this book is to make you a better student, a better citizen, and, some day, a better professional. Ultimately, however, education is not just about how to make a better living. It's about how to make a better life. You can use your college experience now to live better later. This book can help you do that, not because it is Revealed Truth, but because it contains much that is true. The truths it contains, however, won't take you very far if they are only answers to questions on tests. Therefore, it is crucial that you question, consider, and contemplate the issues we have raised. And even that's not enough. To get the maximum benefit from this book you must see how it applies to your life and use it to plan a better one.

CHAPTER 2
Know Thyself

In the 6th Century BC, Socrates advised his fellow Greeks to "know thyself." (This statement has also been ascribed to Thales, an earlier Greek philosopher, and Plato, Socrates' pupil.) We believe the benefits of self-knowledge are as important today as they ever were. Learning about yourself ought to be a primary goal for every student who attends college. Here is why.

We have argued that there are certain qualities of character that significantly influence who will succeed academically and professionally. We make this argument based not on fiction or opinion, but on scientific research.

We assume you want to succeed. Therefore, would it not be useful to know how you stand on those qualities of character which predict success? Moreover, if you'd like to improve your chances for success, you need first to know your current status. How can you find out your "success quotient?"

There is no one way to gain self-knowledge, nor is any route to self-understanding infallible. Certainly, an honest desire to know what you're made of is a good start, but understanding the human psyche is a formidable task. So, while it is an excellent idea to start your quest for knowledge of yourself by looking within as honestly as you are able, it is important to supplement information gained from introspection with information you get from other sources. We've all known people who are blind to their own faults. How do you know you're not one of them? In fact, none of us is immune from picturing ourselves in only favorable ways. It's one of the reasons companies often try to provide 360 degree feedback to their employees. Such feedback comes from all sectors of the organization—subordinates, colleagues, supervisors and customers. It provides a much richer blend of information than the typical performance evaluation which comes from only a single superior. While you're not likely privy to a formal 360 degree evaluation, you can get many of the benefits such feedback provides by informally monitoring others' opinions of you. How do teachers, roommates, pals, best friends, acquaintances, choir directors, teachers, advisors, boyfriends, girlfriends, classmates, teammates, and fellow employees respond to you?

■ Self-Understanding through Testing

Another way to learn about yourself is to take psychological tests and surveys. Such instruments are not fallible either, but they can provide useful information. In fact, many employers require applicants to take a battery of tests before they would consider hiring someone. Examples include: The Dallas Cowboys, The Peace Corps, The Armed Services, and many major corporations. If you attend a selective college, before you were admitted (hired) you had to take a test (SAT or ACT). Before a Medical, Law, Business, Graduate, or Law School will hire (admit) you, you typically have to take the MCAT, LSAT, BSAT, or GRE. Schools and businesses want to be as sure as possible that they're hiring or admitting someone who can perform effectively and will be a good fit for the job and the organization.

There are tests and surveys that measure virtually every human capacity and tendency: Are you infected with TB, cancer, or AIDS? What are your values? With what occupational types do you have the most interests in common? For whom are you likely to vote? What is your personality like? Do you possess the traits and characteristic of successful entrepreneurs? How intelligent are you? Or perhaps, more accurately, what are your strengths in the various kinds of mental abilities which research psychologists have identified?

Medical tests conducted with x-rays or blood analyses tend to be much more accurate than ability tests or personality inventories conducted with paper and pencil. The former are not perfect, however, and the latter do predict behavior better than chance. It has been our observation that students typically make too much or too little of test results. If the results match what they want to hear, they think the test is absolutely on target. If the results are discrepant from their expectations, they dismiss them as utterly worthless.

■ Test Dependability

Here are some basic concepts that will help you to get the most value out of any test you take:

Reliability. A test is reliable to the extent it is stable and consistent. If a person takes a personality test twice, once in September and again in December, the results should be similar—unless the person's personality has changed.

Validity. A test is valid if it measures what it says it measures. A person who scores high on an ability test ought to be able to demonstrate that ability in other contexts. If a personality test indicates high levels of aggression, you would expect the person with the high aggression score to be more argumentative, hostile, or combative on the job than the person with a low aggression score. The College Adjustment Inventory was designed to predict academic success. Some of its subscales are valid for doing so. Other CAI subscales suggest which campus resources are most likely to help a particular student.

Dynamic rather than deterministic universe. Whenever humans are involved, think quantum mechanics rather than simple cause and effect. Humans are probably better likened to the chaotic world of subatomic particles than to the neat world of Newtonian physics. People seldom behave as predictably as billiard balls. Humans exhibit tendencies rather than inevitabilities. There are many factors which contribute to an individual's behavior. We will never know all of them. Smarter people tend to make better grades, but not always. Ambitious students tend to make better grades, but not always. The less gifted student can improve performance by working harder and getting help. The less ambitious student can develop ambition which will have an impact on performance. The brilliant student can be a slacker and flunk out of school.

To summarize, tests and surveys are not crystal balls, but they can provide useful information. They show tendencies, not inevitabilities. You can use the information tests provide to picture yourself more accurately. Knowing where you stand, however, will not improve your performance any more than knowing your temperature will alleviate your fever. If you don't like the picture, you can take action to change your attitudes and behaviors. Doing so will change the results you get, not just on psychological tests, but in school and in life.

■ The College Adjustment Inventory (CAI)

The CAI was developed to identify attitudes, habits, and situational factors that contribute to student success. Students who take the inventory are given scores on five scales:

- ■ Achievement
- ■ Commitment
- ■ Career Planning
- ■ Finances
- ■ Resilience

Three of the scales measure the core personality components of successful students—Achievement, Commitment, and Resilience. There are characteristic ways of thinking, acting, and persisting which lead to success as a student and in a career. The Achievement scale tells you how much you think like successful students. The Commitment scale tells you how much you act like successful students. The Resilience scale tells you how much you persist like successful students.

Achievement. Students with a strong motive to achieve typically have clear goals of moderate difficulty. Their goals are rewarding enough to inspire hard work. The goals are not so difficult to reach that the student is overwhelmed. High achievers think a lot about their goals and the steps that will take them there. They think about the satisfaction that comes with accomplishing something, and they try to avoid the disappointment that comes with failure. They get help when they need it, and they don't wait to be rescued. Instead, they actively seek out expert assistance. Students with a strong motive to achieve are preoccupied with self-improvement. They are eager to address any

personal flaws or weaknesses that would jeopardize their chances for success. They also are preoccupied with overcoming any obstacles or barriers in their path to success. All of these mental habits are characteristic thought patterns of high achievers, day in and day out.

Commitment. If thinking successfully is the starting point for all success, acting successfully is at the heart of it. Of the five subscales on the CAI, this scale better predicts academic success than any other because it measures what students actually do. It should be no surprise to you that successful students study. They attend class, take notes, do homework, read textbooks, and complete their assignments on time.

Resilience. As indicated in Chapter 1, successful people are persistent. They see defeats as opportunities for learning and self improvement. They immerse themselves in constructive action. They believe they possess within themselves the power to influence the outcomes they seek.

Career Planning. Indicates the degree to which students understand their major and have a clear picture of their career path. This scale is typically the easiest to raise because all students have to do to raise it is to investigate relevant majors and careers. A low score does not necessarily suggest low academic performance among freshmen. There are strong indications from other research, however, that confusion about career plans contributes to attrition over time. Think of it this way: most students find school frustrating some of the time. Having a clear career goal based on careful deliberation and accurate information will provide added motivation to cope effectively with the frustration.

Finances. Tells you much you think your financial resources are a hindrance to your success. Anxiety over indebtedness and the need to work long hours to pay for tuition can be obstacles to success. This scale does not measure an aspect of your personality, but rather your perception of your financial status. Again, in the short run, a poor financial score doesn't mean you'll make bad grades. Other studies, however, suggest that financial difficulties can undermine a student's ability to succeed in college.

Percentile Scores. The CAI provides percentile scores. Your percentile score tells you how many people out of one hundred would score lower than you on a particular scale. You are compared with other freshmen who attended Georgia Tech. A score of 58 on Achievement, then, means that 58 percent of freshmen at Georgia Tech scored lower than you on this scale, and 41 percent scored higher. If you attend a school other than Georgia Tech, your responses will be compared to those of students attending a college more like your own.

Significance of Scores. "But what does my score really mean?" Your score predicts your academic performance. By academic performance we mean grades and persistence (Will you return for your sophomore year?). The CAI does not predict your performance perfectly. You're a person, not a billiard ball. As a person, however, your performance is caused by a variety of factors, including most especially those measured by the CAI. A low score suggests you have a smaller chance of making good grades than someone with a higher score. You can, however, use your low score as a prod to action. You can learn to think more like successful students. You can resolve to act more like successful students. You can cultivate psychological hardiness which will make you more persistent. You can investigate career options and get career counseling. You can visit a financial aid counselor and develop a financial plan to assist you in paying for your college education.

We realize that changing your thoughts and habits is not easy. Most things in life that are truly worthwhile are difficult. Thinking and acting successfully and doing so persistently will bring enormous benefits to your life. You will make better grades. Better grades open up the possibility of admission into better professional schools and graduate schools. You will have more opportunities for interesting, challenging work. You will make a lot more money if that is a priority of yours. You will accomplish more in your life.

Chapter 8 tells you more about achievement motivation and how to think like an achiever. Chapters 3 and 4 tell you how to act like a successful student. Chapter 9 tells you how to become more resilient. Chapter 5 tells you how to clarify your career goals. The rest of the book tells you more about the steps you can take to guarantee that you'll get the most out of college and graduate poised for professional success.

■ The Strong Interest Inventory (SII)

The SII measures your interests. This is because people tend to be more successful when they do work that interests them and when they work with people who share many of their interests. The SII tells you first about your general interests. Do you like working more with your hands or with your mind? Would you rather work with things or with people? Next, the SII tells you about your specific interests within those broad themes. If you're a person who enjoys investigating complex problems, do you prefer mathematics, science, or medical science? And finally, it compares you with people who are successfully employed in particular occupations. Are your interests more like the interests of engineers, teachers, or business people?

Why should I take the SII? While the world will not come to an end if you don't take a career test, we think it is useful for you to learn as much as possible about your career identity. Testing is one source of information, and the SII is probably the most researched career test there is. We put the question back to you: why in the world would you not want to learn more about yourself?

■ The Six Themes

Your results on the SII will be presented to you in terms of General Occupational Themes. John Holland, a vocational psychologist, conducted research which indicated that all occupations could be described in terms of six themes. Most careers combine aspects of two or three themes, but others may be described in terms of just one. The six themes are:

Realistic. People who like working with their hands, working out-of-doors, and working with machinery. Basic interests associated with this theme include agriculture, nature, military activities, athletics, and mechanical activities. Occupations high in this theme include carpenters, plumbers, farmers, police, and some types of engineers.

Investigative. People who like working with ideas and using their mind to solve problems. Basic interests include science, mathematics, and medical science. Occupations high in this theme include chemists, mathematicians, physicists, and physicians.

Artistic. People who like working with art, music, literature, and drama. Basic interests include music/dramatics, art, applied arts, writing, and culinary arts. Occupations high in this theme include artist, writer, actor, designer, architect, and illustrator.

Social. People who enjoy working with and for others. Basic interests include teaching, social science, medical service, and religious activities. Occupations high in this theme include teaching, counseling, social work, and coaching.

Enterprising. People who enjoy persuading and influencing others. Basic interests include public speaking, law/politics, merchandising, sales, and organizational management. Occupations high in this theme include sales, management, and entrepreneuring,

Conventional. People who are attentive to detail and like keeping things organized and efficient. Basic interests include data management, computer activities, and office services. Occupations high in this theme include bookkeeping, some types of accounting, and some types of administrative work.

Individuals are generally more satisfied and more successful if they pursue majors and plan careers that are compatible with their interests. Is your current major congruent with your highest Strong themes?

What if my scores are at odds with my current career plan? You might still be successful if you follow that plan. Your interests over time and through experience can gravitate toward the career or major you've chosen. You could also make a significant contribution to a field even though you're a bit different than most other people who populate it. Then again, you might not! You might be heading toward a series of jobs that will frustrate and demoralize you. You do need to ask yourself some tough questions. Do I really know what I'm getting into? Am I doing this for me or for someone else? Do I really know myself as well as I thought I did? It is extremely common for young adults to enter college with a major in mind and end up in a quite different course of study. Most people who flourish in their careers do so because they are interested in the activities associated with that field. Do be wary of entering a field in which you have no interests.

What if I don't have any high scores? It doesn't mean you can't be successful. It does mean that your interests have not yet blossomed in any one area. This could be because you have not yet had enough experience in the world to know what you like. It could be because your interests are spread in moderation across a number of themes. It could also be because you have unrealistic expectations about the world of work and the inevitable challenges and frustrations that accompany any career choice.

What if I have high scores in a number of themes? You have lots of interests. Your challenge is finding a focus. It may be that you will gratify some of your interests at work and others at play. You probably could find satisfaction in a variety of occupations. Accordingly, you can take into consideration even more than other career planners such factors as income, job security, and growth of the field.

■ Personality Type

In the early 1900's, a Swiss psychoanalyst named Carl Jung (1875–1961) developed a personality theory that remains influential today. A contemporary and associate of Sigmund Freud, Jung said, that it is " . . . one's psychological type which from the outset determines and limits a person's judgement." The concept is designed to "deal with the relationship of the individual to the world, to people and things."

In the 1940's, Isabel Myers and her mother, Katharine C. Briggs, developed a test based on Jung's theory for assessing an individual's type preference. Millions of people have taken the Myers-Briggs Type Indicator™ (MBTI) or similar surveys such as the Keirsey Temperament Sorter. You can take a version of the Keirsey on the Internet at http://www.kiersey.com/cgi-bin/keirsey/newkts.cgi .

■ Theoretical Basis for the Keirsey Temperament Sorter or MBTI

In this view of personality there are four continua:

Introversion (I)   vs   **Extraversion (E)**
Preference for primary focus in life, within or without

Sensing (S)   vs   **iNtuition (N)**
Preference for how one takes in information, details through five senses or in larger patterns

Thinking (T)   vs   **Feeling (F)**
Preference for how one decides, based on logic or emotion

Judging (J)   vs   **Perceiving (P)**
Preference for how one organizes one's life, high or low structure

■ Introversion Versus Extraversion

The **I/E** dimension refers to whether your primary focus in life is internal or external. **Extraverts (E's)** are focused outside of themselves on the world of things and people. E's like human interaction and are typically energized by the company of others. They find discussing issues to be useful in reaching important decisions. **Introverts (I's)** prefer relative isolation or the company of one or two rather than a group. Introversion is not synonymous with shyness. I's, however, refresh themselves through reflection and time alone. Because introverts tend to be private people, they may choose only a few friends with whom to be close. Extraverts more likely have a wider circle of friends.

I (Joann) am an extreme introvert, but my career requires me to teach classes, conduct workshops, and give speeches. When I am done I usually feel drained. After making a presentation, for example, I typically seclude myself and rest for a few minutes before going on to other duties. My colleague, Bill, is an extravert and comes back from workshops and public speaking energized. He wants to tell me all about it.

Summary of I/E Dimension

Extraversion	*Introversion*
Social	Private
Expressive	Reflective
Many	Few
Breadth	Depth
Interact	Contemplate
Without	Within
Act first	Think first

■ Intuition Versus Sensing

The **N/S** dimension refers to whether you more likely take in information through your five senses or see larger patterns and meanings. Since the "I" has already been used for introversion, we use the "N" in intuitive to identify this preference. By intuitive, we do not refer to anything mystical. **Intuitive** individuals are focused on the future. They are focused on the big picture. They look for patterns and meanings. They are planners and strategists. They often start projects, then move on and let sensate types complete them. N's are creative. Many great scientists are intuitive. Much of what we value as artistic talent or innovative thinking comes from individuals with a strong N predisposition.

Sensing people gather information through their five senses. They typically want to handle things and look at the facts before making a decision. They also are very practical individuals who make decisions based on experience (history) and the present reality. They have acute powers of observation and a good memory for details. If you are going to need precise directions on how to go somewhere, you want your directions from this person! Working with facts and tangible objects would likely appeal to someone with a strong sensing preference. When talking to an S, give concrete examples to illustrate your concept. You will more likely get your point across.

It is possible to listen for cues to determine another person's preference. Sensing buyers wants to know facts and figures about car performance. Speak to them in their lingo, and you're more likely to make the sale. Intuitive buyers will want to know what options are available and what the value of the vehicle is likely to be in five years. In a job interview, the sensate asks, "What have you done in the past that makes you believe you can handle this job?" The intuitive wants to know, "Where do you believe you'll be in five years?" Three-fourths of the population is sensate.

Summary of S/N Dimension

Sensing	*iNtuition*
Facts	Possibilities
Trees	Forest
Present	Future
Practical	Innovative
Enjoyment	Anticipation
Realistic	Idealistic
Administer	Lead

■ Thinking Versus Feeling

The **T/F** dimension refers to one's preference for basing decisions on logic or emotion. Thinkers tend to make decisions using impersonal, objective judgement—logic and facts. Feelers are more influenced by the impact of the decision upon the individuals involved. Remember, as with the other continua, the people who tend toward a preference for objectivity (thinking types), also have the capacity to feel. And those who make decisions based on personal impact, feeling types, also have the capacity to think. Thinking types think more linearly and can show step-by-step processes by which they arrive at a decision. Feeling types may be less able to specify their rationale, but they can be equally decisive. The difference is that they base their decisions on their emotions and their values. T's often retain information in incredible detail. A thinking type will remember the color of a vase on the mantle and how many forks are in the place setting. A feeling type takes in information in a more global way, remembering vaguely there might have been a fireplace and that the table was pretty. One misunderstanding that often comes up between thinking types and feeling types has to do with emotion. Strong feeling types show their feelings in a more overt way by facial flushes or by blanching, sweaty palms, and a more rapid heart rate. These physiological changes are less apparent in a thinking type. Thus, a strong feeling type may erroneously believe that the thinker has no feelings. However, this phenomenon contributes to a misunderstanding between types. To further confound the issue, there is a gender difference on this dimension. Since about sixty percent of men are thinkers and sixty percent of females are feeling types, you can readily see the potential for conflict. This is why a man might decide on a particular car based on reviews by *Road and Track,* but his wife or girlfriend is more impressed by style and feel.

Is this difference between the sexes socialized or is it biologically based? We don't know yet. Women are certainly socialized to be more nurturing and to care more about feelings (both of self and others). Men who demonstrate strong feelings can be characterized in this society as more eccentric (the passionate artist) or more effeminate. A tendency for feeling also feeds passion, however! Historically, women were denied higher education and discouraged from demonstrating intelligence. Perhaps this accounts for some of the lower numbers of women entering the fields of science and mathematics. Only further research will provide the answers. Note also that the examples above are based on stereotypes. There are certainly thinking women out there (me!) and there are certainly feeling men. Extremes just happen to make better illustrations.

Summary of T/F Dimension

Thinking	*Feeling*
Analysis	Sympathy
Objective	Subjective
Logical	Personal
Critic	Fan
Observer	Participant

■ Judging Versus Perceiving

The **J/P** dimension refers to one's preference for high or low structure. Judging does not mean judgmental, and perceiving does not refer to one's powers of perception. **Judging** people prefer to reach decisions and impose structure in their lives. Judging types often have appointment books and are inclined to be conscientious about time. They are peeved when perceiving types, who live on a time schedule all their own, do not follow through on an obligation. Is a perceiving type going to stop by? Yeah, probably sometime.

Perceiving people want their options left open and often delay reaching a decision. They are slow to organize or plan and must often rush to complete things on time at the last minute. Perceiving types more likely see deadlines as approximations and would rather turn in an excellent report late than a mediocre report on time.

Judging types typically like order and will expend thought and energy to organize their environments. Conversely, perceiving types may be relatively indifferent to the structure of their environment. If you walk into a P's room, order is not a word that immediately comes to mind. If you put a strong judging type in the same dorm room or small apartment with a strong perceiving type, and shake vigorously, you have the makings for a spectacular argument! (It has been our experience that some powerful metaphysical force operates to ensure that J residents are invariably paired with P residents in college dormitories.) The J will unsuccessfully attempt to convert the P into a neatnik. The P will chafe over the J's preoccupation with order. Can negotiations for ground rules be useful? Yes, but both types need to respect the other's tendencies.

The world is made up of about 50/50 judging and perceiving types. There is no "good" or "bad" way to be. You should know, however, that colleges (as well as most workplaces) are generally run by J's who like deadlines and structure. When was the last time a professor told you to turn in your big project whenever you felt like it? But perceiving types are needed too. They do great at jobs where flexibility and spontaneity are necessary. They are the types who like to have their office in their car and set out on a day's appointments knowing they'll do something productive that day, but have no clue what that something is!

Imagine a vacation planned by a judging type and one planned by a perceiving type. How would they differ? By this point, you should have a pretty clear picture of two distinct scenarios.

Summary of J/P Dimension

Judging	*Perceiving*
Closure	Open-ended
Decide	Explore
Structure	Flexibility
Organize	Examine
Proactive	Reactive
Plan	Go with the flow

■ Why Is This Personality Stuff Important to Me?

Understanding yourself helps you better understand what kinds of jobs would suit you. For example, someone with the ST combination (sensing, thinking) might enjoy working with numbers and consider studying accounting. However, the opposite of the ST is the NF. Would an intuitive, feeling individual enjoy working as an accountant? Probably not as much as the ST. The ST individual is very detail oriented and would enjoy detecting the missing dollars on a financial spreadsheet. The NF would more likely prefer to make a notation of "ESP" (error some place) and let it go. That doesn't work well in banks, auditing agencies, and related careers. So, understanding yourself helps you identify which careers match your personality.

Understanding your personality also helps you understand some of your weaknesses. Every type has strengths, and every type has weaknesses. Many companies administer an MBTI or an equivalent type of personality inventory so they can use the information to build teams. Team composition based on personality type is useful because management can devote a comprehensive array of strengths to a project. If every member of a team in an S, the group will get the details but might miss the big picture. If every member of a team in an N, there is a danger of losing the details.

Personality type can help you communicate better with your professors. PhD's are typically research scholars first and so are often introverts. They may be more comfortable with one person in their office than speaking to a large class. A strong interest in research does not ensure outstanding communication skills. You may have to work hard to identify yourself as a person in trouble and in need of some of their attention.

What else can you know about type that can help you connect with your profs? You can listen to them for cues. Do they talk as sensing or intuitive types? Are they more detail oriented, or is their focus on the big picture? You would be well served to write answers to exams that connect with the personality type of the professor.

Another way you can use this information on type is to know yourself better. If you are a strong P, you may struggle with deadlines and details. It's in your interest to get sufficiently well organized to meet your academic and financial obligations. You can choose to do what you must to get that degree, even if it is slightly uncomfortable now and again.

And don't forget that your parents, your friends, and your boss have personalities, too. If you understand personality more, you can understand others, as well as yourself.

There are 16 possible combinations of the four continuums. Your combination is just as good as anyone else's. Each of the 16 combinations has strengths and weaknesses. If you understand your personality type, you can interview more effectively, contribute more to teams of which you're a member, and probably even get along a little better with your roommate. Please refer to the following charts for information about your type and the workplace and occupational choice.

Typical Work Stressors

Extraverts	vs.	Introverts	Thinking Types	vs.	Feeling Types
Working alone		Working with others	Using personal experience to assess situations		Analyzing situations objectively
Having to communicate mainly by e-mail		Talking on the phone a lot	Adjusting to individual differences and needs		Setting criteria and standards
Lengthy work periods with no interruptions		Interacting with others frequently	Noticing and appreciating what is positive		Critiquing and focusing on flaws
Having to reflect before taking action		Having to act quickly without reflection	Focusing on processes and people		Focusing on tasks only
Having to focus in depth on one thing		Too many concurrent tasks and demands	Using empathy and personal values to make decisions		Being expected to use logic alone to make decisions
Getting feedback in writing only		Getting frequent verbal feedback	Having others react to questioning as divisive		Asking questions that feel divisive

Sensing Types	vs.	Intuitive Types	Judging Types	vs.	Perceiving Types
Attending to own and others' insights		Having to attend to realities	Waiting for structure to emerge from process		Having to organize selves' and others' planning
Having to do old things in new ways		Having to do things the proven way	Being expected to use "inner timing"		Working within time frames and deadlines
Having to give an overview without details		Having to attend to details	Too much flexibility around time frames and deadlines		Other's distrust of last-minute energy
Looking for the meaning in the facts		Checking the accuracy of facts	Having to marshal energy at the last minute		Having to finish and move on
Focusing on possibilities		Needing to focus on past experience	Staying open to reevaluations of tasks		Developing contingency plans
Too many complexities		Being required to be practical	Dealing with surprises		Being required to plan ahead

Personality in the Work Place

Extroversion vs. Introversion

Extroversion:
- Like variety and action
- Tend to be faster, dislike complicated procedures (especially ES types)
- Are often good at greeting people (especially EF types)
- Are often impatient with long, slow jobs done alone
- Are interested in the activities of their job, in getting it done, and in how other people do it
- Often do not mind the interruption of answering the telephone (especially EF types)
- Often act quickly, sometimes without thinking it through
- Like to have people around (especially EF types)
- Usually communicate freely (especially EF types)

Introversion:
- Like quiet for concentration
- Tend to be careful with details, dislike sweeping statements (especially IS types)
- Have trouble remembering manes and faces
- Tend not to mind working on one project for a long time and uninterrupted
- Are interested in the details and/or ideas behind their job
- Dislike telephone intrusions and interruptions (especially IT types)
- Like to think a lot before they act, sometimes without acting
- Work contentedly alone (especially IT types)
- Have some problems communicating to others since its all in their heads (especially IT types)

Thinking vs. Feeling

Thinking:
- Like analysis and putting things into logical order
- Can get along without harmony
- Tend to be firm minded
- Do not show emotion readily and are often uncomfortable dealing with people's feelings (especially IT types)
- May hurt people's feelings without knowing it
- Tend to decide impersonally, sometimes paying insufficient attention to people's wishes
- Need to be treated fairly in accordance with the prevailing standards
- Are able to reprimand people impersonally, although they may not like doing so
- Are more analytically oriented--respond more easily to people's thoughts (especially IT types)

Feeling:
- Like harmony
- Efficiency may be badly disrupted by office feud
- Tend to be sympathetic
- Tend to be very aware of other people and their feelings (especially EF types)
- Enjoy pleasing people, even in unimportant things
- Often let decisions be influenced by their own or other people's personal likes and dislikes
- Need praise and personal attention
- Dislike, even avoid, telling people unpleasant things
- Are more people oriented--respond more easily to people's values

Sensing vs. Intuition

Sensing:
- Like focusing on the here and now and reality
- Rely on standard ways to solve problems and dislike problems in which this approach doesn't work
- Like an established order of doing things (especially SJ types)
- Enjoy using and perfecting skills already learned more than learning new ones
- Work more steadily with realistic idea of how long it will take (especially ISJ types)
- Reach a conclusion step by step (especially ISJ types)
- Are patient with routine details (especially ISJ types)
- Are impatient when the situation gets complicated (especially ES types)
- Are not often inspired and rarely trust the inspiration when they are
- Tend to be good at precise work (especially IS types)
- Create something new by adapting something that exists

Intuition:
- Like focusing on the future and what it might be
- Like solving new problems in unusual ways and dislike solving routine problems
- Dislike doing the same thing repeatedly (especially NP types)
- Enjoy learning a new skill more than using it.
- Work in bursts of energy, powered by enthusiasm, with slack periods in between (especially ENP types)
- Reach an understanding quickly (especially ENP types)
- Are impatient with routine details (especially ENP types)
- Are patient with complex situations (especially IN types)
- Follow their inspirations, good or bad, regardless of the data (especially with inadequate type development)
- Frequently make errors of fact, preferring instead the big picture
- Dislike taking time for precision (especially En types)
- Create something new through a personal insight

Judging vs. Perceiving

Judging:
- Work best when they can plan their work and follow the plan
- Like to get things settled and finished
- May decide things too quickly (especially EJ types)
- May dislike to interrupt the project they are on for a more urgent one (especially ISJ types)
- May not notice new things that need to be done in their desire to complete what they are doing
- Want only the essentials needed to begin their work (especially Esj types)
- Tend to be satisfied once they reach a judgement on a thing, situation or person

Perceiving:
- Adapt well to changing situations
- Prefer leaving thing open for alterations
- May unduly postpone decisions (especially IP types)
- May start too many projects and have difficulty fishing them (especially ENP types)
- May postpone unpleasant jobs while finding other things more interesting in the moment
- Want to know all about a new job (especially INP types)
- Tend to be curious and welcome a new light on a thing, situation, or person

Occupational Trends

	Introverted and Judging	Introverted and Perceptive	Extroverted and Perceptive	Extroverted and Judging
Intuitive with Thinking	**INTJ** Scientific or technical fields Computers Law Or any other occupations where they can use their intellectual creativity and technical knowledge to conceptualize, analyze, and get the task done	**INTP** Scientific or technical fields Or any other occupations where they can use their solitary, objective analysis of problems based on their technical expertise	**ENTP** Science Management Technology Arts Or any other occupations where they have the opportunity to take on new challenges continually	**ENTJ** Management Leadership Or any other occupations where they can use tough-minded analysis, strategic planning, and organization to get the task done
Intuitive with Feeling	**INFJ** Religion Counseling Teaching Arts Or any other occupations where they can facilitate emotional, intellectual, or spiritual development	**INFP** Counseling Writing Arts Or any other occupations where they can use their creativity and focus on their values	**ENFP** Counseling Teaching Religion Arts Or any other occupations where thy can use creativity and communication to help foster the growth of others	**ENFJ** Religion Arts Teaching Or any other occupations where they can help others with their emotional, intellectual, and spiritual growth
Sensing with Feeling	**ISFJ** Education Health care Religious settings Or any other occupations where they can draw on their experience base to personally help people in a behind-the-scenes manner	**ISFP** Health care Business Law enforcement Or any other occupations where they can use their gentle, service-related attentiveness to detail.	**ESFP** Health care Teaching Coaching Childcare worker Skilled trades Or any other occupations where they can use their outgoing nature and enthusiasm to help people with their practical needs	**ESFJ** Education Health care Religion Or any other occupations where they can use their personal concern to provide service to others
Sensing with Thinking	**ISTJ** Management Administration Law enforcement Accounting Or any other occupations where they can use their experiences and attention to detail to get the task done	**ISTP** Skilled trades Technical fields Agriculture Law enforcement Military Or any other occupations where they can use their hands-on, analytical work with data or things	**ESTP** Marketing Skilled trades Business Law enforcement Applied technology Or any other occupations where they can use their action-oriented focus to attend to the necessary details	**ESTJ** Management Administration Law enforcement Or any other occupations where they can use logic and organization of the facts to get the tasks done

Characteristics Frequently Associated with Each Type

	Sensing Types		Intuitive Types	
Introverts	**ISTJ** Quiet, serious, earns success by thoroughness and dependability. Practical, matter-of-fact, realistic, and responsible. Decide logically what should be done and work toward it steadily, regardless of distractions. Take pleasure in making everything orderly and organized--their work, their home, their life. Value traditions and loyalty.	**ISFJ** Quiet, friendly, responsible, and conscientious. Committed and steady in meeting their obligations. Thorough, painstaking, and accurate. Loyal, considerate, notices and remembers specifics about people who are important to them, concerned with how others feel. Strive to create an orderly and harmonious environment at work and at home.	**INFJ** Seek meaning and connection in ideas, relationships, and material possessions. Ants to understand what motivates people and are insightful about others. Conscientious and committed to their firm values. Develop a clear vision about how best to serve the common good. Organized and decisive in implementing their vision	**INTJ** Have original minds and great drive for implementing their ideas and achieving their goals. Quickly see patterns in external events and develop long-range explanatory perspectives. When committed, organize a job and carry it through. Skeptical and independent, have high standards of competence and performance--for themselves and others
Introverts	**ISTP** Tolerant and flexible, quiet observers until a problem appears, then act quickly to find workable solutions. Analyze what makes things work and readily get through large amounts of data to isolate the core of practical problems. Interested in cause and effect, organize facts using logical principles, value efficiency.	**ISFP** Quiet, friendly, sensitive, and kind. Enjoy the present moment, what's going on around them. Like to have their own space and to work within their own time frame. Loyal and committed to their values and to people who are important to them. Dislike disagreements and conflicts; do not force their opinions or values on others.	**INFP** Idealistic, loyal to their values and to people who are important to them. Wan an external life that is congruent with their values. Curious, quick to see possibilities, can be catalysts for implementing ideas. Seek to understand people and to help them fulfill their potential. Adaptable, flexible, and accepting unless a value is threatened.	**INTP** Seek to develop logical explanations for everything that interests them. Theoretical and abstract, interested more in ideas than in social interaction. Quiet, contained, flexible, and adaptable. Have unusual ability to focus in depth to solve problems in their area of interest. Skeptical, sometimes critical, always analytical.
Extraverts	**ESTP** Flexible and tolerant, they take a pragmatic approach focused on immediate results. Theories and conceptual explanations bore them--they want to act energetically to solve the problem. Focus on the here-and-now, spontaneous, enjoy each moment that they can be active with others. Enjoy material comforts and style. Learn best through doing.	**ESFP** Outgoing, friendly, and accepting. Exuberant lovers of life, people, and material comforts. Enjoy working with others to make things happen. Bring common sense and a realistic approach to their work, and make-work fun. Flexible and spontaneous, adapt readily to new people and environments. Learn best by trying a new skill with other people.	**ENFP** Warmly enthusiastic and imaginative. See life as full of possibilities. Make connections between events and information very quickly, and confidently proceed based on the patterns they see. Want a lot of affirmation from others, and readily give appreciation and support. Spontaneous and flexible, often rely on their ability to improvise and their verbal fluency	**ENTP** Quick, ingenious, stimulating, alert, and outspoken. Resourceful in solving new and challenging problems. Adept at generating conceptual possibilities and then analyzing them strategically. Good at reading other people. Bored by routine, will seldom do the same thing the same way, apt to turn to one new interest after another.
Extraverts	**ESTJ** Practical, realistic, matter-of-fact. Decisive, quickly move to implement decisions. Organize projects and people to get things done, focus on getting results in the most efficient way possible. Take care of routine details. Have a clear set of logical standards, systematically follow them and want others to also. Forceful in implementing their plans	**ESFJ** Warmhearted, conscientious, and cooperative. Want harmony in their environment; work with determination to establish it. Like to work with others to complete tasks accurately and on time. Loyal, follow through even in small matters. Notice what others need in their day-by-day lives and try to provide it. Want to be appreciated for who they are and for what they contribute	**ENFJ** Warm, empathetic, responsive, and responsible. Highly attuned to the emotions, needs, and motivations of others. Find potential in everyone; want to help others fulfill their potential. May act as catalysts for individual and group growth. Loyal, responsive to praise and criticism. Sociable, facilitate others in a group, and provide inspiring leadership	**ENTJ** Frank, decisive assume leadership readily. Quickly see illogical and inefficient procedures and policies, develop and implement comprehensive systems to solve organizational problems. Enjoy long-term planning and goal setting. Usually well informed, well read, enjoy expanding their knowledge and passing it on to others. Forceful in presenting their ideas.

■ Personality Type & Life's Activities

1. My major/career choice: _____

2. My MBTI/Keirsey type: ____ ____ ____ ____

3. Typical careers for my type: _____

4. Advantages of my type for my career: _____

_____

_____

5. Challenges for my type in my career: _____

_____

6. Strengths of my type as a student: _____

_____

7. Challenges of my type as a student: _____

_____

8. Strengths of my type as a leader: _____

_____

9. Challenges of my type as a leader: _____

_____

10. Strengths of my type as a team member: _____

_____

11. Challenges for my type as a team member: _____

CHAPTER 3
Organizational Skills

Image courtesy of Digital Vision.

So, you say you're serious about success. How about checking your "SQ," your Success Quotient? We know a pretty fool-proof method of determining your SQ. How you spend your time is a very reliable indicator of just how serious you are about success. Do you spend most of your waking hours pursuing goals which will turn your dreams into reality? Then, your SQ is high. Do you spend a lot of time watching TV, playing computer games, and hanging out in the mall? Then, your SQ is low (unless you're running for Slacker of the Year). In fact, if you want a painfully honest look at yourself, monitor your time in 15 minute increments for a week. How much of what you do, day in and day out, will result in academic and professional success?

Another way to think about your time is as an investment. People commonly dream of wealth. What do they do to create it? Do they invest their money wisely, or do they spend it frivolously? Just about anyone can create wealth IF they regularly invest modest portions of their income in a mutual fund. It takes time and discipline to create wealth, but there is no magic formula for doing it. (If you'd like to learn how you can guarantee YOUR financial future, take a look at *The Millionaire Next Door*.) It also takes time to create success, and neither is there a magic formula for producing it. In what activities do you invest your time? Will those activities produce success?

You've probably heard the expression that "time is money." Every day you are given 1440 minutes. You have to spend a certain amount of them on eating and sleeping and other basics, but you have a lot of discretion about what you do with the rest. Do you invest your daily allotment of minutes in such a way that you'll reach those goals which create your success? Obviously, you need to determine what those goals are before you can evaluate how effectively you invest your time. Choosing goals can be a daunting task for an entering college student. In fact, we suggest that one of your collegiate goals should be to start clarifying your life's goals and selecting a career direction.

Until you have done so, there are some safe goals you can run with: making good grades, clarifying a career plan, developing your capacity for leadership, and maintaining your health and physical fitness. These goals are not yet SMART (**s**pecific, **m**easureable, **a**ction oriented, **r**ealistic, and **t**imely), but if you accurately monitored your activities for a week, you could make a pretty good judgment whether what you did would help you get a 4.0 GPA, career focus, charisma, and an Olympic tryout.

If a 4.0 GPA seems unduly ambitious and an Olympic tryout seems ridiculously out of reach, you'll want to substitute your own particular goals in the categories above. In fact, it's not a great idea to make goals too high. Research by David McClelland consistently found that the highest achievers were those who set goals of moderate difficulty. Neither, however, is it good to set goals that provide no challenge. You've doubtless heard of the expression "killing time." It's doing nothing. It's aimlessness. It's a life with no challenges, a life of low goals. Reflect for a moment on what it really means to kill time. If time is our most precious commodity, killing it is, in effect, committing suicide in small increments.

Getting organized and managing time is really about reaching goals. Your goals, in turn, are a reflection of who you are, what you stand for, what your mission in life is. That's why time management is so important. Yes, it's good to turn work in on time so you won't lose points on an assignment or get fired from a job. But, what time management is really about is keeping yourself on track to realize your potential. In other words, time management is self management.

Consider the following analysis of tasks in terms of their importance or value and their urgency or time sensitivity. Everything you do can be classified as of higher or lower importance. It can also be classified as more or less urgent. Remember, though, just because something is urgent doesn't mean it's important. Indeed, a common problem is to be tyrannized by the urgent.

Stephen Covey, in *The 7 Habits of Highly Effective People*, stresses the importance of spending as much time as possible in Cell III of the following diagram, the Important, but non-Urgent category. You shouldn't spend much time in frivolous activities such as those found in Cell IV. Nor should you spend a lot of time in Cell II doing non-essential things just because they're time sensitive. Naturally, as crises arise (Cell I) you address them, but if you live much of your life in Cell III you won't have as many crises.

According to Covey, effective people are proactive. They plan for their future and invest in it every day by spending significant amounts of time doing things of value to their success as they define it. They know what their priorities are and organize around those priorities. They plan their work and then work their plan. It would follow that

Tasks Importance		
	(+)	**(−)**
Task Urgency **(−)**	I Crises Today's big project Tomorrow's exam	II Phone rings TV show in 5 minutes
(+)	III Planning Next month's big project Final exam in 7 weeks	IV Reading junk Video games surfing

highly effective students study regularly and seldom cram. This enables them to get good grades without a lot of stress. Consistent study means fewer late-nighters and no all-nighters. There is still time for rest and relaxation and recreation. There is just not a lot of wasted time.

SMART Goals

Achievers are goal-directed. Good time managers organize their time and resources to reach goals. But what goals? We can't tell you which goals to pursue, but we can help you define them in such a way that you'll more likely reach them. While there is nothing wrong with aspiring to excellence, realizing potential, accumulating wealth, and finding true love—none of these is a goal you can place on your To-Do list or enter at the 2 PM slot for Wednesday.

*Let's take "aspiring to excellence." Is it SMART? Clearly not. It is neither **S**pecific, **M**easurable, nor **A**ction-oriented. Since it is so vaguely defined, it's difficult to know whether it's **R**ealistic or not. And it does not appear to be **T**imely. Let's say, however, that you are an ambitious person and truly do aspire to excellence. But what kind? Athletic, political, academic, or something else? For the sake of the argument, let us further assume that it is the intellectual arena in which you desire to excel. Some day you hope to be an outstanding research physician—maybe even win the Nobel Prize. This means getting top grades to get into a top medical school. Your SMART goal for the term might then be to make no less than a 3.5 GPA, including an A in Chemistry. We don't know whether this is realistic for you or not, but it is timely (this term), specific (a particular GPA), and measurable (GPA can be calculated). It's not yet action oriented, but it's not hard to make it so. Students make good grades by attending class, studying long hours, forming study groups, getting tutoring, and using effective learning techniques. Any of these steps could be entered into your planner. For example, you could plan to attend your daily Chemistry class and weekly lab, study chemistry daily for two hours, and post a notice on a bulletin board in the Chemistry Building expressing your desire to study with other serious students.*

Now, how could you set a SMART athletic goal? Or a SMART romantic one?

Our experience has been that most college students haven't been pushed very hard when they were in high school. Accordingly, they didn't need to be very organized or disciplined. Now that you're in college, it's time to get down to business. We've already suggested that the key to success is to stay focused on what has the most value. What is the best way to stay on task?

■ Weekly Schedule

We believe that most students will profit from some intermediate and longer term planning. As a freshman, that means you should plan your week and your term to help you stay focused on what is important. Consider the weekly schedule on page 35. The student—Sally Schein—is taking calculus, chemistry, computing, English, and a freshman seminar in Psychology. She wants to become an engineer, but isn't sure which branch to major in—probably mechanical or civil. The core courses are the same for most science and engineering majors, so she doesn't need to decide yet.

Sally has scheduled 22 hours of study time. This is a LOT more than she studied in high school, but less than she's been advised. Sally had a cousin who attended the same school that Sally is attending, and he flunked out because he didn't study enough. That definitely got her attention, and she entered school determined to succeed. She thought this amount of study time was a reasonable compromise, and she could adjust it up or down depending upon how the semester goes.

There are other principles which are at work in this schedule. Notice that Sally has spread out her study times throughout the day and throughout the week. Research has clearly established that individuals learn more by distributing their periods of study over a day's time rather than lumping all their study times together. In other words, if you were to study three hours a day, you'd get more out of it if you studied an hour in the morning, an hour in the afternoon, and an hour at night than if you studied from 8–11 PM in the evening. Notice also that she has given herself Friday night and all day Saturday off. If it were the week before finals, she could study during that time, but we recommend giving yourself a period free of academic responsibility if you can manage it. Another feature of Sally's schedule is that work comes before play. It is very common for students to waste time during the day and finally start to buckle down about 9 PM, if not much later. The trouble with this practice is that you are, in effect, punishing yourself for playing rather than rewarding yourself for working. Nearly one hundred years of research psychology supports the notion that work gets easier when followed by a reward. So, study first. Then reward yourself with relaxation and recreation. Another reason why long late-night study sessions fail is because most people are tired and sleepy at that time. Accordingly, they are less productive, and the whole process leaves a bad taste in their mouth. Small wonder they don't like to study, don't like school, and don't enjoy learning. What a terrible mindset to cultivate in an era in which life-long learning is an imperative for success.

The key then is to put first things first. As a student, your first commitment should be academic success. We believe one of the best ways to stay on track is to create a reasonable weekly schedule and stick to it.

It is also helpful to look at time from a longer term perspective. Businesses often have five-year plans. Some organizations project their futures for ten years or even longer. It was reported in the news a while back that Japan had a national strategic plan that stretched out over 50 years! It is unlikely that the average freshman is clear enough about the future to make long range plans. It is possible, however, to plan for the school term, be it quarter or semester.

Weekly Schedule

	MON	TUES	WED	THRUS	FRI	SAT	SUN
8 AM						Sleep in	Sleep in
9 AM	English		English		English	↓	↓
10 AM	Calculus	Calculus tutorial	Calculus	Calculus tutorial	Calculus	Free	Free
11 AM	Study	Study	Study	Study	Study		
12 PM	Lunch	Chem tutorial	Lunch	Lunch	Lunch		
1 PM	Chem	Lunch	Chem	Misc	Chem		↓
2 PM	Relax	Computer Science	Misc	Computer Science	Study		Study
3 PM	Study	Work out	PSY 1000	Study	Work out		Study
4 PM	Work out	Study	Study	Work out	Misc		
5 PM	Study	Dinner	Relax	Misc	Relax		
6 PM	Dinner	Computer Science Lab	Dinner	Dinner	Dinner		↓
7 PM	Study	Relax	Relax	Chem Lab	Free		Study
8 PM	Study	Study	Study	Chem Lab			Study
9 PM	Free	Study	Study	Chem Lab			Study
10 PM		Free	Free	Free			Relax
11 PM	↓	↓	↓	↓	↓	↓	
12 AM							

■ Semester Schedule

In high school, most of your projects were very short term. You studied for tomorrow's test, or maybe today's. You wrote tomorrow's paper. In college, projects are often larger in scope and also more complex. There are also multiple projects to manage at the same time. It is not possible to excel if you're always in a time crunch, struggling to meet deadlines, with no time for quality, deliberative work. Take a look at Sally's semester schedule. She must read about 1800 pages of textbook material—an average of 120 pages per week. Some weeks are more demanding than others. For example, during week 4, she has a quiz, a test, a computer program to write, and an English paper due. During week 13, she must take a test or complete a project in each of her five classes. She cannot do justice to all of them if she waits until the last minute to get started.

Sally made out her semester's schedule by going over the syllabus in each of her classes. This enabled her to have the "big picture" of what the semester would include. Many planners have daily and monthly calendars for you to fill out. You will do yourself a favor if you consult your course syllabi and transfer key due dates to your planner. We strongly recommend scheduling start-up dates for bigger projects as well. For example, if you have a major paper due November 1, a good strategy to follow would be to make a note in your planner to get started on October 15. Once you've gotten started you can better estimate how much time you need to schedule to work on the paper over the two weeks which follow your start-up time.

■ Daily Schedule

To manage your time effectively, we believe it is imperative that you use a planner. You can buy a fancy leather one with lots of features for $50 and more. You can also do quite nicely with a $5 spiral notebook planner found in your college bookstore. The big thing is to use it. Enter important events on the appropriate dates. Schedule start-ups for big projects. Use the big picture—the semester's due dates—to drive what you do each day. We strongly recommend making out a To-Do list. You can make it out on Sundays in anticipation of the week to come, adjusting it daily according to changing demands. Or you can make it out in the morning as you plan how you will attack your day. Some people like to make out their to-do lists the last thing in the evening in anticipation of the following day. The important thing is for you to identify important tasks every day. It's a good idea also to prioritize these tasks. If today is the last day you can apply for financial aid, turning in that application gets top priority. If you're a pre-med student taking organic chemistry, studying for tomorrow's midterm gets a very high priority.

The purpose of all this planning and goal setting is not to complicate your life, but to simplify it. YOU are in charge of your life. Your planner is a tool to help you manage your time and your life effectively. You use this tool to keep yourself on task, moving towards those goals that comprise your success. Perhaps the greatest business theorist of the 20th Century was Peter Drucker. He states that a plan isn't a plan if it's not on paper. Other efficiency experts say that if you fail to plan, you plan to fail. So, get a planner and start planning.

■ Working Your Plan

If the road to hell is paved with good intentions, the road to mediocrity is paved with plans not followed. It accomplishes little to transfer due dates from your syllabi to your planner if you don't complete the work that will enable you to meet your deadlines.

Semester Schedule

Course and requirements	Week 1	Week 2	Week 3	Week 4	Week 5	Week 6	Week 7	Week 8	Week 9	Week 10	Week 11	Week 12	Week 13	Week 14	Week 15
Psychology 5 Quizzes 4 Projects 200 pp. Text		Quiz			Quiz	Career Rsrch		Quiz	Teach Class		Quiz	Resume	Professional Report	Quiz	
Calculus 7 Quizes Midterm Final Exam Homework 300 pp. Text	HW	Quiz HW	HW	Quiz HW	HW	Quiz HW	Mid Term Exam	Quiz HW	HW	Quiz HW	HW	Quiz HW	HW	HW	
Chemistry 3 Tests Labs Final Exam 500 pp. Text				Test		Lab Report	Test					Test	Lab Report		
Computer Science 3 Tests 7 projects 300 pp. Text		Program	Test	Program		Program	Test	Program		Program		Program	Test	Program	
English 2 Tests 2 Papers Final Exam 500 pp. Text				Paper			Test					Paper	Test		

How do you cultivate the character to follow your plan?

Working hard is, to a great extent, a habit. If you're not used to doing the hard work it takes to meet challenging expectations, you may feel some pain at first. Think of it as similar to getting into physical shape. If you've never run five miles before, it would be impossible to do so while maintaining a brisk pace. It IS possible, however, to alternate jogging and walking at a much slower pace however for five miles or at least one mile. On subsequent days, you'd spend more time jogging and less walking. Gradually, you'd extend the distance covered. In less time than you'd think, you'll be covering the five miles at a respectable pace.

If you're not used to studying 15–30 hours per week, the process of acclimating yourself to such a regimen is similar to training for distance running. Every day you put in your hours. Initially, you'll probably deviate from your schedule. You'll probably find that it's difficult to concentrate on schoolwork for extended periods of time. It's OK to take some study breaks. With practice your patience and concentration will grow. Here are some hints which will help you stay on task:

1. Make out a To-Do list every day. If you miss a day, resume the list the next day.
2. Prioritize it.
3. Monitor it. There is something about checking off completed items that is very reinforcing.
4. Find a distraction-free place to study, and go there when you're scheduled to study. Many students find the library to be a productive place.
5. Identify your biggest time-wasters such as net-surfing, video games, and TV watching and put yourself on a strict diet. Allow yourself time on one of these activities only after you've done school work for a reasonable amount of time.
6. Join a Study Group comprised of students who are serious about success. Members don't have to be brilliant nor do they have to be total grinds, but they need to aspire to academic success.
7. Work first, then play.
8. Tackle your most challenging or least preferred work first. Get it out of the way. After that, everything else will seem easier.
9. Try to get as much studying done between classes as you can.
10. Figure out what your long term goal is, e.g., becoming a physician. Remind yourself that your daily small tasks fit into your master plan. You may find it helpful to put your name, followed by M.D. on a post-it. Display it prominently where you study to remind yourself what you're really up to.
11. Finally, if nothing else works, talk with a counselor.

■ Planning for Life

We're not against good luck, but we think it usually comes to those who have their act sufficiently together to take advantage of the available opportunities. One of the best ways we can think of to make yourself luckier is to assume absolute and total responsibility for your own future. Whether you want wealth, challenging work in an exciting field, or the chance to make a contribution to society, it's up to you to get there. Your future doesn't just happen. You create it. Of course, it's true that you have personal and historical limitations. Shaquille O'Neill and Cindy Crawford were endowed with natural assets that most of us can only dream about. It makes a difference whether you were born during an economic boom or a depression, during peacetime or war. It also matters that you'll be launching your career(s) in the Information Age. And it's different being born into wealth and privilege than into poverty and oppression. Still, it's up to you to determine your future, regardless of the hand life has dealt you.

In 1953, graduating seniors at Yale University were asked about their future plans. Not surprisingly, these elite young men and women had many lofty aspirations. Only a small percentage of them, however, had plans on paper. Some years later it was those individuals who had fleshed out their plans on paper while still in college who turned out to be the most successful.

We've stated earlier that it's difficult for someone just out of high school to make long-range plans. Traditional-age freshmen (18–19 years of age) simply have not had enough experience to develop the insights needed to plan for the long haul. We still believe planning is a very useful experience. For a few dollars and some time, you might find a visit to the following Web site to be helpful: *http://www.demon.co.uk/mindtool/lifeplan.html*. There, you can engage in an electronic life-planning venture.

We have also laid out a four-year plan (see Master Plan below) to help you become an outstanding graduate. The Master Plan is neither sacred nor etched in stone. It is an example of the sort of comprehensive planning we're talking about. If you start managing your time and your life now, you will accomplish light years more than you ever thought possible. Perhaps by your senior year you'll have a plan on paper to rival that of the highly successful 1953 Yale graduates.

THE MASTER PLAN

The citizen of the 21st Century will think globally and plan strategically. You can start preparing right now by mapping out your strategy for getting the most out of college. Here is our Master Plan for using college as a springboard to success in the Information Age. Use it as a rough guide for creating your own plan.

■ Freshman Year

Your first mission is to immerse yourself in the academic enterprise. Get organized. Become a serious student. Acquire basic computer skills. Begin to identify majors and careers of interest. Learn to manage stress. Start networking.

Develop Organizational Skills

Establish weekly schedule.

Identify semester deadlines.

Use To-Do list; prioritize and monitor daily.

Master use of a planner.

Develop a file system for school work and personal information.

Organize an effective work space.

Develop Learning Skills

Learn how to use the library.

Review material regularly.

Learn effective reading, writing and note taking techniques.

Get to know your professors.

Learn where to access old tests.

Master Computer Skills

Organize your hard disk.

Know e-mail.

Master a word processing program.

Learn spread sheet software.

Learn mathematics software if needed.

Stress Management Skills

Develop an exercise program.

Maintain a healthy diet and good sleeping habits.

Learn to relax & keep perspective.

Go Global

Learn a language.

Investigate "language house" living arrangements.

Read about international events.

Attend events sponsored by International Students Association

Get Involved

Join a campus organization.

Start Networking

Connect with professors.

Connect with alumni.

Connect with people in field of interest.

Connect with students who share your interests.

Find Direction

Do a thorough self-assessment.

Determine compatibility of majors with your interests and abilities.

Explore various career fields.

Investigate coursework required for different majors.

Get career counseling as needed.

Get advisement.

Explore co-op and internships.

Create resume disk.

■ Sophomore Year

You use your organizational, learning, computer, and stress management skills throughout your collegiate career. You declare a major and begin to consider electives. You join a professional organization and contribute to it. You develop job search skills and secure career-related employment.

Declare Major

Plan a schedule for taking required course work.

Get to know your advisor.

Look for electives that are compatible with your interests and complement your major.

Join Professional Association

Join student chapter affiliated with your major and/or career choice.

Attend local meetings regularly.

Be as active as your schedule allows.

Develop contacts by attending national meetings, conferences and/or seminars when convenient.

Periodically, read over trade journals associated with your major/career.

Expand Network of Contacts

Maintain current network.

Develop new contacts.

Use a Rolodex™ or other filing system

Enhance Computer Skills

Learn graphics/presentation software.

Go Global

Live in a language house.

Get Career-Related Experience

Start Co-op or internship.

■ Junior Year

You assume more active and responsible positions in your extra-curricular activities. You cultivate contacts on and off campus. You learn more about your fields of interest. You find out about graduate and professional schools.

Evaluate Chosen Field

Keep up with your field through contacts and trade journals.

Talk to your professors and employers.

Refer to career-related material in your library, counseling center and career services office.

Check out job qualifications necessary in your field.

Continue co-op/internship.

Research Graduate or Professional Schools of Your Choice

Determine the benefits of an advanced degree in your field.

Identify strong graduate programs.

Apply for graduate or professional school entrance exams.

Continue Leadership Development

Enhance skills in communications and management.

Attend Leadership workshops and seminars.

Run for office or assume responsibility for a project.

Develop contacts for mentoring and possible job leads.

Go Global

Select a Study Abroad program.

Keep Up With Computing

Learn key software applications.

■ Senior Year

You're almost there! Apply for graduate programs and take entrance exams if you plan to get an advanced degree. Gear up for the job search by revising your resume and preparing for interviews.

Take Graduate or Professional School Entrance Exams

Check campus resources for available preparatory programs.
Check bookstores and library for preparatory books.

Arrange for Interviews Through Campus Career Services Office

Attend programs explaining procedures of Career Services office.
Follow all procedures carefully.
Cultivate and maintain good relationship with key staff.
Take advantage of job search seminars and workshops.

Revise Your Resume

Detail skills or experience using the STAR Technique.
Tailor your resume to the company or graduate school you are interviewing.
Also create strong generic resume suitable for Web sites and data bases.

Get References

Decide who can give you the strongest references.
Talk to references about possible job leads.
Inform your references about your strongest selling points.
Supply references with copy of your resume.

Apply to Graduate Schools or Look for Permanent Employment

Tap network of contacts.
Don't limit job search to campus recruiters.
Look for opportunities to develop new skills in learning organizations.
Develop strategy for expressing match with company or graduate school.

Master the Interviewing Process

Research typical questions and develop effective answers.
Prepare effective questions to ask the interviewer.
Send thank-you notes to each interviewer.

Take Plant Trips or Visit Grad Schools

Investigate what happens during the plant trip or in the graduate school selection process.

Send any requested additional information.

Evaluate Offers

Determine what your needs are versus what the company or graduate school has to offer.

Seek guidance, if necessary.

Choose the best offer.

■ Managing Data

While I was working on a collegiate success book some years ago I lost the hardcopy of the chapter I was working on. Neither could I find the disk that contained the chapter. I launched an archeological dig through the various strata that covered my desk and the piles of artifacts that had accumulated around my office. I also foraged through my briefcase and scoured my office at home. For a while I feared I would have to rewrite the entire chapter, a process that appealed to me about as much as getting a root canal without benefit of anesthesia. Eventually, I found the lost document and the missing disk. They had been in my office all along. Ironically, the chapter covered the topic of organizational skills.

I mention this anecdote to illustrate that disorganization is costly. My episode with the lost chapter cost me time, energy, and stomach lining. I resolved at that time to organize my data more effectively. It is something I continue to struggle with. I am not by nature a neatnik. I will say, however, that I have not lost any more chapters, and I do find that keeping chaos at bay helps me get more done with less effort.

■ Getting Started

First, you need some tools. For starters, your campus bookstore will have small portable file boxes made of plastic or heavy cardboard. If you're really strapped for cash, you can get by with a cardboard box. We recommend, however, that you bite the bullet and get a real file cabinet—at least a two drawer model. Get some manila folders, and you're in business.

Create a file for each class you take. Some you'll purge at the end of the term, but it's a good idea to save course materials in your major. We also recommend creating a few personal files for Finances, Campus Activities, Car, Taxes, and the like. You'll soon find that your file cabinet is getting full.

We also recommend that you create an office for yourself. If you live on campus, your room will be furnished with a desk. With an organized desk and an organized file cabinet you've got an office. It's probably a good idea to visit an office supply store and pick up a few other tools. There are vertical file holders and desk drawer organizers. A glass jar or plastic cup works fine to hold pencils and pens. See the list of office supplies that are used by some students somewhere, some of the time. You won't need every one, but you should equip yourself to be an effective student.

Finally, if you can afford a computer, we urge you to get one. It will be vastly easier to complete your work. It will also be easier to correspond with your professors and fellow students. The point we wish to make here, however, is that you should also keep your computer organized. Create a file for class work, with a subfile for each class. Get a disk organizer for disks. Back up your hard drive with disk copies.

OFFICE SUPPLIES

Pencils	*Highlighter*
Pens	*Stapler*
Eraser	*Staple Puller*
3-Ring Binder	*Planner*
Felt Pen	*Hole Punch*
Colored Pens/Pencils	*Ruler*
Manila Folders	*Post-Its*
Address/Phone Book	*Tape*
Computer	*Index Cards*
Computer Disks	*Calculator*
Printer	*Spiral Notebooks*
Notebook Paper	*Dictionary*
Printer Paper	*Thesaurus*
Scissors	*Style Manual*
Graph Paper	*Card File*
Paper Clips	*File Cabinet*

Even with an organized filing system, you may find yourself swimming in a sea of cellulose. Naturally, you want easy access to important papers without having to sort through useless garbage. Here are two hints to make your system work: 1. When it comes to paper, practice the OHIO system: Only Handle It Once. Use it, file it, or trash it. 2. When in doubt, throw it out.

■ Summary

1. The speed and change that will characterize the 21st Century demand good organizational skills. This means YOU have got to get organized.
2. Set goals and determine the activities that will help you reach those goals.
3. Plan your time for the quarter or semester.
4. Establish weekly and daily schedules.
5. Prioritize every day.
6. Create an office.
7. Develop a file system.
8. Keep class material organized.
9. Organize your computer.

■ Organizational Habits Self-Assessment

T   F   1. Most days I make out a To-Do list.

T   F   2. I use a planner almost every day.

T   F   3. I have entered key due dates and test dates from my course syllabi into my planner.

T   F   4. I typically meet deadlines for projects.

T   F   5. I start on projects and study for tests in plenty of time to do solid work.

T   F   6. I have a file cabinet or box to store classwork and other important documents.

T   F   7. I could easily find the important papers and documents in my room.

T   F   8. The hard drive on my computer is well organized.

T   F   9. I keep my computer disks well organized.

T   F 10. I have created a "home office" which is an effective place to study.

T   F 11. I have most of the office tools I need to be an effective student.

T   F 12. I maintain a weekly and/or semester schedule.

Give yourself one point for each item you could honestly answer as True. The more points you have, the better organized you are.

Name: _____ Date: _____

■ Goal Setting Exercise

1. List a goal to reach by the time you graduate:

_____

List steps to reach your goal:

1.a _____

_____

1.b _____

_____

1.c _____

_____

2. List a goal to reach by the end of the semester:

_____

2.a _____

_____

2.b _____

_____

2.c _____

_____

3. List a goal to reach within one week:

_____

3.a _____

_____

3.b _____

_____

3.c _____

_____

CHAPTER 4
Learning to Learn

Image © PhotoDisc, Inc., 1996.

While you already possess some learning skills or you wouldn't be in college, chances are good you could improve them. One way to improve them is to cultivate learning skills which are based on core proven principles. Research psychologists have studied learning for many years. Here are some of the principles they have identified.

Motivation Matters

One of the oldest principles in psychology is the Law of Effect. Organisms behave in order to get results. Rats, for example, will learn to negotiate a maze in order to get food. The late B. F. Skinner studied "operant conditioning" or "instrumental learning" for many years at Harvard. He found that he could reinforce learning in animals by rewarding them with food after they behaved in some specified way. In fact, Skinner even succeeded in teaching pigeons to play ping pong! Complex organisms like humans can behave in complex ways to get results. The results toward which humans strive can also be complex. While small children might learn to tie their shoes for a reward of a cookie, there are not many college students who expect their physics professor to dispense candy bars for mastering quantum mechanics. Why does a college student struggle to solve a difficult calculus problem? Or stay up to write a strong essay on the American economic system? The answer varies according to the student, but the important point is that motivation is extremely important. Motivation comes from getting some sort of reward.

Rewards can be tangible: My parents will buy me a car if I make A's, or I'll get to keep my scholarship if I maintain a B average. They can also be intangible: I'll have prestige if I get a degree from a top school, or maybe I'll finally win my parents' approval. Rewards can also be extrinsic (e.g., money) or intrinsic (e.g., work that interests me). Humans are complex, and so are their motives and the rewards that activate those motives.

In order for you to learn, you must be motivated to do so. You probably have a variety of motives for attending college. (Remember the discussion in Chapter One of why students attend college.) You will learn best if your motivation is strong. Your motivation will be strong if you are clear on what rewards you seek. If you are like most students, you have a variety of rewards which motivate you. The more these rewards are consistent with your values, personality, and self-image, the stronger will be your motivation. Intrinsic rewards tend to be the most powerful: Some students practice musical instruments because of their love for music, some immerse themselves in great literature because they are drawn to it and others spend hours solving difficult problems because their passion is engineering. It is a lot harder to work for things that reward your parents than it is to work for things that reward YOU.

Rewards which are essential for survival are also powerful. Unless you can count on inherited wealth, you will have to work for a living. As an educator it should come as no surprise to you that I encourage learning. Regardless of my opinions, however, education is an enormous asset to career success. In our knowledge-based economy, people with college degrees generally have much higher incomes, more job security, and more flexibility than those who never attended college. While formal education unfortunately is not synonymous with learning, there is a connection. You must learn in order to get your degree.

A motivated learner learns more. You will maximize your chances for educational success when you find ways to motivate yourself. What are the reasons you're in college? They should be the sources of your motivation.

■ Practice Makes Perfect

One of the phenomena that has been extensively studied is memory. Memory comes in two versions: short term and long term. Short term lasts for seconds. Individuals can generally commit 7 + or − 2 bits of information to short term memory. Long term can (but doesn't always) last a lifetime. One key for academic success is to get the important stuff transferred from short term to long term memory. There are some classic studies that show how quickly memory can fade. Reflect on the following studies and determine their implications for improving your learning effectiveness.

Ebbinghaus Study of Nonsense* Syllables	
Time Elapsed	*Per Cent Remembered*
20 minutes	53 %
2 days	31 %
15 days	25 %
31 days	22 %

Spitzer Study of Textbook Retention	
Time Elapsed	*Per Cent Remembered*
1 day	54 %
7 days	35 %
14 days	21 %
21 days	18 %
28 days	19 %
63 days	17 %

The trend is the same in both these studies. Memories fade rapidly at first. Gradually, one starts to forget less. Of course, there is less to forget after awhile. If we graphed the rate of forgetting it would look something like this. The Y or vertical axis represents memory. The X or horizontal axis represents time. Note that just after completing an effective study session, memory/mastery is high. The student knows enough to make an A. After a few weeks, represented by moving to the right on the horizontal axis, the student has forgotten much of what was learned. If the student took a test, performance would be poor. The student then has to relearn much that was forgotten quickly the night before the test. If there is a lot of material, the student will have a difficult time.

Why would a researcher study the memory of nonsense syllables? Nonsense syllables are more likely equivalent IN MEANING among subjects. Regular English words vary in their relevance to different learners. For example, poets might more readily recall words such as sonnet, limerick, and verse. Computer programmers might more readily recall words such as bit, byte, disk, and flow chart. What relevance might this have for students wanting to learn? The hardest part of learning comes at first, when the learner has no context. If you work hard enough to gain a context, additional learning will come easier. Another way of putting this is: The more you know, the easier it is to learn new information. An implication of this is: Be an information junkie. Become a life long learner. If your goal as a student is to learn as little as possible, just enough to get by each test, then you are dooming yourself to become a lifelong second class citizen. We live in the Information Age. If you're not informed, you're not very powerful or very marketable. In fact, you are at risk of becoming marginalized in our society. Another implication is: Be patient. Trying to learn a lot of new material will be tough at first. Expect some frustration. IF you learn to cope with frustration and hang in there, you will gradually acquire more and more knowledge. That means you'll have an ever expanding context which will make learning ever more stimulating and enjoyable. You will also find that it will be easier to learn.

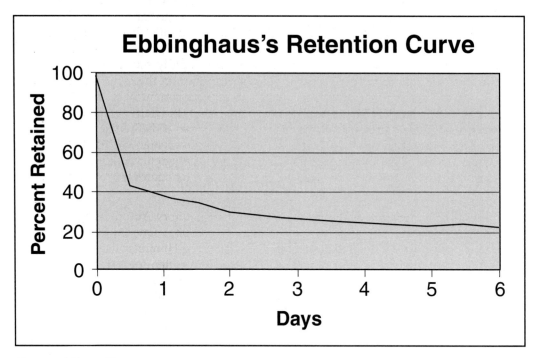

Curve of Forgetting

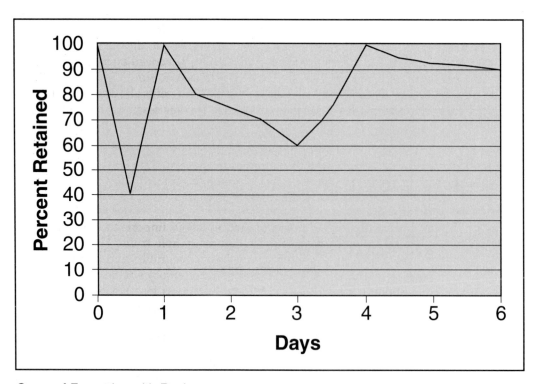

Curve of Forgetting with Review

The problem every student has, then, is how to remember material for the big test? The answer, of course is PRACTICE, which is just another word for REVIEW. Look again at the above graph which describes a student's changing mastery of material over time. The student studies and obtains a relatively high mastery of the material. Of course, as soon as studying is over, forgetting rapidly sets in. But note what happens when the student reviews the same material later on the same day. Very quickly the material is recalled. And then, something really important happens. THE RATE OF FORGETTING SLOWS DOWN! This is represented by the flatter slope of the line representing forgetting after each review session. The slope of the line gets progressively more flat, which is to say that regular review sessions move material from short term to long term memory. Additionally, note the slope of the learning curve. It becomes steeper after each successive review, which is to say that learning comes more readily each successive time one goes over the same material.

Here's another way to think about memory. You're hungry, and you want pizza. You look up Joe's Pizza and phone in a number. One minute later your mouth may already be watering in anticipation of the Extra Humongous size anchovie and jalapeno pizza you've ordered, but you've already forgotten Joe's Pizza phone number. Let's suppose Joe's pizza is so good that you order another pizza the next night. Again, you look up the number. You keep doing this every night, and after a while you don't have to look up the number. You're also overweight, developing high cholesterol and running out of money, but that's another story. By practicing, which is to say reviewing, you've memorized the number to Joe's Pizza.

■ Distributed Practice Makes More Perfect

Assume you wanted to learn something. It could be tennis, calculus, or the lines to a play. Assume further that you were willing to devote three hours per day to accomplish this goal. Would you learn more if you practiced an hour in the morning, an hour in the afternoon, and an hour in the evening OR would you learn more if you practiced (or studied) three hours every afternoon? In general, you would develop competency more rapidly if you practiced in three one-hour sessions than if you practiced in one three-hour session.

■ Meaning Matters

Motivation and Practice are indisputably important truths in developing an approach to effective learning, but are they the whole truth? They are not. There is another psychological approach which emphasizes cognition and meaning. Individuals are best able to learn things they understand. Rote memory will take you only so far. Moreover, while people will learn in order to get good grades or parental approval or admission into medical school, people will also learn because they are inherently curious. Humans are not content to memorize; they want to understand. When they understand a subject, they are better able to relate new material to it. They are better able to apply their learning to solve real world problems.

Connections and organization help individuals to learn. Which is the easier shopping list to follow?

I

Steak, carrots, milk, potato chips, roast, lettuce, cheese, corn chips, fish, onions, butter, pretzels, shrimp, turnips, yogurt, nuts

II

MEAT	PRODUCE	DAIRY	SNACKS
steak	carrots	milk	potato chips
roast	lettuce	cheese	corn chips
fish	onions	butter	pretzels
shrimp	turnips	yogurt	nuts

The second list is easier to recall because it's organized into manageable chunks. Organization provides structure and meaning. Simply organizing material into categories is not enough to help you become a master learner. You must also be able to make connections. If the study of history is merely the rote memorization of dates and kings and presidents, then it is not very useful unless you're on a quiz show or taking a poorly designed history test. If, however, studying the causes of wars in the past helps policy makers and citizens to understand the causes of wars today, it becomes extremely useful (and therefore also rewarding).

■ Active Learning Beats Passive Learning

You will learn more from solving calculus problems than from watching somebody else solve them. This isn't to say that you can't learn vicariously from watching your professor solve a problem on the board. It is to say that you'll be shortchanging yourself if you plan to restrict your learning to reading, watching, and listening. Research suggests that active note takers get more out of class than students who do not take notes. Similarly, active readers retain and comprehend more than passive readers. Harvard's Thomas Perry conducted research on reading comprehension and found that the best readers were extremely active and analytical when they studied a document. Instead of reading a passage from beginning to end, they were constantly asking questions of the text, organizing it into meaningful categories, and relating text material to other knowledge they possessed. They jumped around within the body of text they were reading. Passive readers could compete with active readers on simple tests of factual recall, but they were unable to perform on a par with their more active reading peers on tests that called for comparing and contrasting, drawing conclusions, relating new material to old, and synthesizing novel solutions. Since work and life rarely consist of knowing the answers to quiz-show type questions, it is important to cultivate active reading habits.

■ The Neural Basis of Learning

Well informed people are able to acquire new information more readily than poorly informed people. In the world of knowledge, it's a matter of the knowledge-rich getting richer and the knowledge-poor getting left progressively farther behind. In recent years, scientists have significantly advanced our understanding of the human brain. They have discovered the physiological basis for the fact that knowledgeable people are able to learn more readily than less knowledgeable people. People who are active learners have many more pathways connecting their neurons than people who know less. More pathways create more possibilities for acquiring new knowledge. Throw some information at an active learner, (s)he'll have lots of facts to relate to the new information. An inactive learner will have a harder time connecting the new information to anything.

As active learners age they are likely to stay mentally alert longer than inactive learners. If Alzheimer's disease impairs some of the brain's pathways, the active learner has many more pathways to call on. Putting it bluntly, dense people have a hard time acquiring knowledge. As they age, what little knowledge they have will erode. This does not appear to be a pleasant prospect.

Neural connections are differentially formed in the human brain according to the mode of input. We can take in information by sight, sound, touch, or smell. Smell and the closely related sense of taste aren't typically useful in academic settings (unless you're studying at the Culinary Institute of America, the *real* CIA). Learners will have more neural connections going for them, however, if they create graphic images of material they study to supplement the lectures they hear and the words they read. As mentioned earlier, actively solving mathematical problems enhances learning over watching the professor solve them.

■ Anxiety and Learning

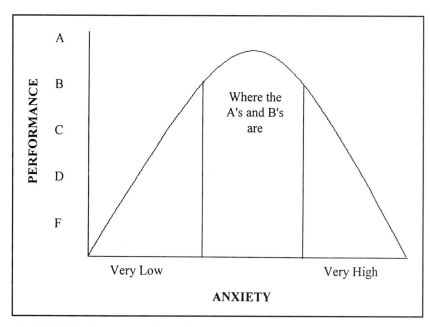

Anxiety & Performance Graph

What is the relationship between anxiety and learning? Common sense might suggest a simple linear relationship: zero anxiety leads to maximum learning and performance. Maximum anxiety leads to zero learning and performance. Like many things, the relationship between these variables is more complex. If one were to graph the relationship, it would be curvilinear. With NO anxiety, the learner is lethargic or asleep. Learning is minimal. With high anxiety, the learner is distracted by the symptoms of anxiety and fears of failure. A little anxiety is just fine. The learner will, in effect, be more motivated to learn and more attentive to the material to be learned. As depicted in the graph above, it is generally the moderately anxious student who makes the A's and B's.

Another part of the anxiety/performance relationship is that anxiety impairs performance the most dramatically when the task is complex. You could be very frightened and still remember your name and phone number. You might not, however, be able to recall all your new vocabulary words from your Conversational Chinese class or be able to balance difficult equations in Organic Chemistry. Since college consists of mastering progressively more difficult material, it is important for students to learn how to manage their anxiety. You have two choices: 1. Control the anxiety. 2. Control the complexity. See Chapter 10 on Stress Management for more information on how to keep your anxiety in the productive zone. You really don't have much choice about the complexity of the material that is presented to you. Or do you?

If you want to be an investment counselor, you have to learn Finance. If you want to go to medical school you have to do well in Organic Chemistry. If you want to be an engineer, you must understand Calculus. Your professors will choose the textbooks you read and the homework you are assigned. They will make up the tests you take. There is, nonetheless, a way for you to have some influence over the complexity of the material you must master. If you learn material really well, it will seem less complex and difficult than material with which you have only a passing familiarity. Brain surgery would be impossibly complex for the person on the street. For the trained and experienced surgeon, however, it is just another day at the office. By using all the principles outlined in this chapter, you can gain a relative mastery of subjects you must learn. If you are motivated, organize your material, stress understanding rather than rote memorization, and review it regularly—it won't seem so complex. When you have to perform under pressure and within time constraints on a difficult exam, you will be less vulnerable to anxiety.

Based on well established principles of learning, a student who wants to be an effective and efficient learner would observe the following guidelines:

The Rules of the Road for Student Learning

1. Find a way to motivate yourself. Why are you in college? What are your goals? How will this subject help you?
2. Review regularly. Review the most important material. (This implies that part of the student's task is to figure out what's important.)
3. Spread your studying time out over the day and the week.
4. Organize your material into meaningful categories. Relate new knowledge to old. Strive to understand. Don't settle for rote memorization.
5. Learn actively. DO THE HOMEWORK! Employ different modes of learning— pictures as well as words, sights as well as sounds, numbers as well as narratives.
6. Exercise patience and a little faith. Trust that knowledge accumulates. The more you know, the easier it is to learn.
7. Inoculate yourself against anxiety by learning important material extremely well.
8. Manage your time. Prioritize your work. Work your priorities. Use a planner. Organize projects into component parts. Then do each part (From Chapter 3).

Learning Challenges

1. Given the general principles covered in this chapter, what is the best way to maximize learning from textbooks?
2. How can a student maximize in-class learning?
3. Given the general principles covered in this chapter, how can you get the most out of class notes?
4. What is the best way to get the most out of homework?
5. How can a student profit the most from review?
6. Design a comprehensive and effective system of study.

■ Learning and Your Campus

While the principles of learning outlined above hold true in any setting, you will have to apply them in a particular situation—the college you attend. Colleges and universities come in all shapes and sizes. They can be private or public, religious or secular, large or small, two-year or four-year. There are many other factors as well that characterize a college and impact the type of experience you will have. Here are some of them.

Teaching Versus Research

Colleges vary widely according to how much research is emphasized. Community colleges typically exist exclusively to educate their students. Some Liberal Arts Colleges emphasize research and some don't. Research universities are expected to create new knowledge through research as well as educate their students. Community college teachers typically teach three to five courses each term. Professors at research universities teach fewer courses, but are expected to conduct research as well. At some universities, professors spend much more of their time doing research than they do teaching. Their focus is on creating new knowledge and publishing their findings in scholarly journals. In order to conduct research, faculty may have to spend long hours preparing grant applications for funding which keeps labs running and pays graduate student stipends. Professors are more likely to be promoted and get better pay raises for doing good research than for being a great teacher. Spending time with freshmen isn't rewarded nearly as well as getting a grant to pay for expensive lab equipment. They may focus more on their graduate students than on their undergraduates. There may be very little incentive for them to invest their time and energy in advising and mentoring freshmen. Teaching Assistants, typically graduate students, may do much of the teaching. They're concerned about THEIR research. They won't graduate unless they finish their theses and dissertations. This may be the first time they've ever taught.

This doesn't mean that you will get better teaching and advisement at a non-research university, but that may well be true. On the other hand, there are some clear benefits that go with the research university:

- Your professors are more likely to be on the cutting edge of their field. When they conduct their research, they are ideally pushing the frontiers of knowledge. As new developments occur in their field they are more likely to be acquainted with them than their non-research oriented colleagues.
- If your professors are conducting original research, chances are good that they are connected with government and industry research agencies. Your professors' connections can be your bridge to this world where contacts are made, internships secured, and careers started.
- Chances are good that laboratory equipment and facilities are up-to-date.
- The library is probably larger and its holdings more extensive.

All of this is to say that there are many opportunities available to you at a research university, but it's up to you to seize them. Help is probably available, but it probably won't seek you out. If you want it, you can get counseling, tutoring, and help planning your career—but you've got to go get it. One of the biggest challenges at a research university is to find a way to form good working relationships with your professors. Remember, their focus is often first on their research and second on their graduate students' research. Only after attending to these concerns do they focus on their undergraduate students. Moreover, some may be introverted scholars whose love for the complex and the abstract may make them seem remote and aloof to you. It's still to your benefit to make a connection with your professors. It's an even bigger advantage to cultivate a strong connection with some. Here are some ways to do so.

- Attend classes.
- Take notes.
- Ask questions.
- Take advantage of a professor's office hours. These are hours when (s)he is committed to being available for consultation with students.
- Participate in departmental committees and task forces within your major. You'll get to know professors in your field and vice versa.
- Consider working on campus for the academic department in which you major. Even though much of the work may be menial, if you do it conscientiously, consistently, and well you'll impress your employers.
- Become an undergraduate research assistant. This is probably the best way to connect with a researcher — helping to conduct the research. You'll learn about the field and you'll learn about the researcher. If you have aspirations to go to graduate school, this is the route for you.

■ More about Professors

College professors are typically different from high school teachers. They have typically spent more years undergoing formal education. Many have doctorates, typically a PhD. This suggests a broad understanding of their general field — physics, psychology, literature — and a relative mastery in a specialty. In order to get a PhD, they probably got a Master's degree first during which time they wrote a thesis (a really big paper). In order to get their PhD, they had to pass exams demonstrating comprehensive knowledge of their field. Finally, they had to conduct original research and defend it before a committee comprised of PhD's in the field. Some dissertations are hundreds of pages long. Most scholars took anywhere from four to eight years AFTER college in order to complete their Master's and PhD. Given the nature of their graduate school experience, it is not surprising that many professors are more focused on their field of study than on their students.

Once aspiring academics become PhD's, they try to secure a position with a college or university. They start out with the rank of Assistant Professor. They have five to seven years to get tenure. Tenure means a promotion to Associate Professor and also considerable job security. It amounts to a virtual life-time contract with the university. Tenure is a HUGE deal in the lives of many professors. If they don't get it, they are asked to leave. They typically get it by (you guessed it) conducting research. The more prestigious the university, the higher quality will be the research expected. Assistant professors are under a lot of pressure. They may be teaching classes which are new to them. I once had a young professor ask me how best to avoid students since they were impeding his ability to get his work done.

Let's suppose that things go reasonably well for a hypothetical Assistant Professor. Her research is successful, and she guides her graduate students through their dissertations. She participates in academic committees, and her teaching is evaluated favorably. Tenure is granted along with the rank of Associate Professor. She would like, however, to continue progressing in her academic career. She wants to become a Full Professor. She will accomplish that goal by doing more of the same. She must produce more research. In some fields, she'll have to produce a book or two. Assuming she becomes a Full Professor, she'll have more power in the department and may be asked to serve on committees whose work affects the entire institution. Once she becomes a Full Professor, a process which may take ten or more years, she can relax a little. Of course, by now she may be very busy coordinating research and committee responsibilities. Moreover, many universities have instituted a policy of post-tenure review to ensure that tenured professors don't rest on their laurels. They are expected to remain highly productive.

■ Commuter Versus Residential Campus

Some campuses have housing on campus for their students, and some don't. There are some students who commute to school even though their schools have on-campus housing. Students typically commute because it's cheaper for them and their parents if they live at home. Non-traditional aged students (over 25) are also more likely to commute.

You should be aware that there are major advantages to living on campus.

- Research shows that college has a more profound impact on students who live on campus than those who commute.
- It's closer to the library.
- It's easier to join a study group.
- It's easier to get involved in a campus organization, and that's where a lot of your education will occur.
- It's easier to make it to campus events: football games, concerts, speeches, job fairs, etc.
- It's easier to form friendships with classmates when you're around them 24 hours a day.
- You will more likely talk about the meaning of life with your roommate at 2 AM than with your family over the dinner table.

Finances may prevent you from living on campus, but your commuter status does NOT have to impair your educational experience. Here are some steps you can take in order to get the most out of college even if you're there only part time.

- Join at least one study group and become an active participant.
- Join at least one campus organization and become an active participant.
- Attend an occasional campus event.
- Don't be a PCP student (one whose only contact with campus is that they arrive at the **P**arking lot, walk to the **C**lassroom, and back to the **P**arking lot).
- Plan to spend at least one extended period of time each week in the library researching your papers and studying.

■ Size Matters

The private liberal arts college I attended had just 600 college students and no graduate programs. When I started graduate school, it was at the University of Texas with approximately 35,000 students. Today, the University of Texas at Austin enrolls about 50,000. Both experiences were very positive, but they were very different. At Southwestern, it was easy to feel at home. I roomed with my best friend from high school. I quickly learned the names of virtually every student and professor. At Texas, I knew a miniscule percentage. At Southwestern, the president knew my name. At Texas, in four years, I never once saw the president. I was married and a parent by the time I entered graduate school, but I occasionally wondered what it would have been like to be a freshman there—a nameless number among the thousands of other 18–19 year-olds. It is very easy to feel isolated on a large campus, but connections and alliances have a great deal to do with whether or not you return as a sophomore. This is true first of all because you must feel at home to get the most out of your college experience. Additionally, it is through your classmates that you are able to get class notes when you're too sick to get out of bed. It is with your classmates that you form study groups. We've mentioned earlier that it's very important to form good working relationships with your professors. This can be a daunting task on a large campus. Review once more the recommendations for how to connect with professors at a research university. The principles that help commuters connect with a campus also work for residential students. Use those principles to your advantage.

■ Summary

1. Find some reasons for attending college. Use these reasons to motivate you to study.
2. Daily and weekly review pays huge dividends in academic performance.
3. Spread your studying out over the course of the day and the week.
4. Emphasize understanding over memorization.
5. Practice **active** learning. Take notes, ask questions, analyze textbooks, do homework, draw comparisons between one body of knowledge and another.
6. The more you learn, the easier it gets.
7. A little anxiety never hurt anybody. A lot does. Control anxiety by mastering material.
8. You will get more out of college if you connect with your professors.
9. The best way to connect with professors is generally through their fields of study.
10. It's up to you to initiate contact with your professors.

■ Devising Effective Learning Strategies

This chapter discusses five principles based on well established research which facilitate student learning:

1. **Motivation**
2. **Review**
3. **Distributed Practices**
4. **Organization and Meaning**
5. **Active Learning**

1. Using these principles, devise a system for getting the most out of your textbooks within your own time constraints.

2. Using these principles, devise the maximally effective system for taking class notes and learning the most from them.

3. Using these principles, devise a system and schedule of study which is highly efficient and effective.

CHAPTER 5
Career Planning
Navigating the Unknown

Why are you in college? Most students have gone to college for the past 20 years for career-related reasons. Students say better jobs at better pay, more than anything else, is why they're in school. We know that students have other motives for attending school, and we certainly applaud those who strive for enlightenment, self understanding, and personal development. Still, it's hard to focus on truth if you're worried about paying the bills. The cost of a college education continues to soar—well over $100,000 for a degree from an elite, private school. The state university that employs us estimates that an in-state student will have to spend about $50,000 for a bachelor's degree. That includes room and board and books. It's probably a conservative estimate, and Georgia Tech is regarded as one of the great bargains in all of higher education.

A college degree is a big expenditure. It's also a big investment in your future professional success. How can you make sure your investment is sound? It's a chaotic time to plan a career. Times are chaotic because change is constant. Rapid technological change creates waves that ripple throughout society and throughout the job world. The good news is there are a number of strategies which can help you succeed in the 21st Century.

■ Find Your Niche

The first strategy is not, in fact, new. In general, you will be more successful and find more satisfaction if you work in a field that matches your interests and abilities. Choose a field that fits you. In order to do so you must know yourself well enough to have a good understanding of your interests and abilities. You must also be sufficiently familiar with the job world to know which field will suit you. If you've taken the College Adjustment Inventory, your Career Planning subscale score is an indication of how proactive you've been in this domain. If you got a low score, it is easy to raise it by taking some of the constructive steps that are described below.

■ Know Thyself

You will understand yourself better to the extent that you engage the world and reflect honestly upon that engagement. In other words, try things on for size and think about the experience. Take different classes. Read different books and periodicals. Attend different speeches. Get involved in different activities. Hang out with different kinds of people. Eat different kinds of food. Listen to different kinds of music. Go to different kinds of movies. Don't restrict yourself to what you've always done, what's familiar and comfortable. College is a time to examine yourself and explore the world. While cultivating a pioneering spirit in self-exploration is probably the best step you can take at this stage of career planning, there are other strategies which can help.

■ Career Exploration Exercises

College Catalog Exercise. You can use your college catalog in a structured way to advance your vocational self-understanding. Go through your school's catalog and read the statement of purpose of each major division. (Divisions are usually called Schools or Colleges, as in "School of Business" or "College of Engineering.") Now, go back and read the statement of purpose of each department in each division that interested you. Next, identify and list the required courses that go with each department that intrigued you. Look up the course descriptions. Eliminate the departments with courses that don't appeal to you. Investigate further the departments with requirements that you think would interest and challenge you. Check out suggested elective courses. Talk with a departmental representative. Question some seniors who major in the department. Go to the campus bookstore and thumb through some introductory and advanced textbooks. By now, you will have narrowed down your list of departments to a more manageable number.

But don't stop now! Do some more research. How marketable is a particular major? What careers does it prepare you for? Find out. Read up on it. Check with Placement or your campus Career Center. Would I be good at it? (I might be interested in astronomy, but unless I'm a whiz at mathematics, I'd never make it through all the physics.) Take an introductory course. See if it matches your interests and abilities.

Self-Assessment Exercise. Take four sheets of paper. Draw a horizontal line across the middle of three of them. On the top half of the first, list those classes that you have liked or excelled in. On the second page, list preferred hobbies and activities. On the third, jot down any jobs you have held. What tasks did you perform in each job? List them. Now, on the bottom half of each page list the interests, values, and abilities suggested by the classes, activities, and tasks.

Now, look at the bottom half of each page for patterns and commonalities. Distill those common traits into a vocational self on the fourth page. The major you declare and the career you choose should be as compatible as possible with your vocational self.

■ Use Campus Resources

Most colleges have Career Centers or Counseling Centers staffed by professionals whose mission is to help you plan a successful career. You can get counseling, testing, computer aided guidance, and career information. These services cost substantial sums of money to the customer who seeks them in the private sector, but most colleges provide these services for free.

■ Know the World

How many of you would agree to marry someone sight unseen? OK, it's a dumb question. Mail-order brides and arranged marriages belong to another time and place. You certainly wouldn't rely exclusively on gossip or propaganda about another person before you took the big plunge. You'd want some objective information. And you'd definitely want to spend some time with this person first.

We believe that choosing a career is at least as important as choosing a mate. Yet we find an incredible number of people who are willing to settle for mail-order majors or arranged careers. No wonder there's so much job dissatisfaction out there. Know what you're getting into.

Most majors acquaint you with a field. They don't necessarily prepare you for a job. Employers hire people to fill particular jobs. The more knowledgeable you are about jobs that match your needs and skills, the more likely you are to find the right one for you. You will also more likely convince an employer to hire you.

Just about the best way to find out about career opportunities is to get some career-related work experience before you graduate. Reading about something is never as revealing as trying it on for size. Additionally, you can discover things like how a particular company treats its employees or how the different divisions of a corporation work.

Obviously you've got to have some inkling of a career goal before you can look for career-related work. But what if you're really up in the air about your future? What should you do then? And is there any general information about today's job world that you should know?

If you're thoroughly confused, get counseling. Also, do the College Catalog and the Vocational Self-Assessment exercises described above. As important as it is to know your vocational self, though, it is equally important to know something about the job world.

Find the Career Information Library on your campus. It's probably in the Counseling Center or at the Career Services office. If your college doesn't have a career library, you should be able to find plenty of information in the main library. Look over the Occupational Outlook Handbook. You can also find the OOH on the web at <http://stats.bls.gov/ocohome.htm>. Check out any occupations that intrigue you. What sort of work is involved? What about pay and other benefits? What kind of training is required? Will you need additional degrees in order to advance? What does the future hold for the field? It's all in the Handbook, but don't stop there. You can find a wealth of career related information on the web. Many professional societies have Web sites, as do many corporations. It's also a good idea to participate in a student professional society, and it's advisable periodically to read pertinent trade journals.

One of the best ways to find out about different kinds of work is through people who do the various jobs. Informational interviewing and networking are buzz words among professionals today and for good reason. You can learn about a career from professors and staff, from relatives and friends of the family, through your fraternity or sorority, at your church, mosque or temple, from alumni, and at your own job. All you need is the gumption to ask. People like to talk about themselves, so most will be glad to discuss their work with you.

■ Conducting an Informational Interview

First, do your homework. Get an overview of the career you're investigating by reading up on it. It's presumptuous to expect a professional to teach you about the basics. Besides, if you know something about a field, you can ask much better questions. More intelligent questions not only get better information, they also make you look good. And if you come across as a serious, thoughtful person who is genuinely interested in success, the person you're interviewing will probably not hesitate to recommend you to others in the field. They can provide you with additional information and may be the start of your network of professional contacts. (How about that? You thought you were simply finding out about a career, and you're already building a network!)

Another reason you want to make a good impression is that this person might be able to hire you for an internship next summer. Or give you a strong lead to someone else who might hire you or give you your first job after you graduate.

The other bit of homework you need to do before the interview is on yourself. Your contact will be able to give you more relevant information if he knows whom he's talking to. We recommend developing an oral resume. This is a short summary of your vocational interests, values, skills, and experiences. You give it early on in the interview, before you ask your questions.

■ Oral Resume of Janet Smith

Dr. Score, an industrial psychologist at Acme Enterprises, has just ushered Janet in to his office. "So you think you might be interested in industrial psychology, " he says. "What would you like to know?"

"A little bit of everything, but first I want to thank you for taking the time to talk with me. I'd also like to tell you a little about myself and how I got interested in the field, if it's all right with you. Dr. Schwartz said you could help me better if you knew a little about me."

Dr. Score smiles and nods for Janet to go on. She leans forward in her chair and begins.

"I'm a freshman at State U., and I'm majoring in psychology. I've always gotten along well with people—in school and band and church. But I've also been really curious about what makes people tick. I can remember watching *Awakenings* one night on TV and being fascinated. After that I thought I wanted to be a psychiatrist. I read about Freud and Jung. I tried to figure out what my dreams meant and what everybody's hang-ups were.

"Then, my senior year I took a psychology course and learned that there was more to psychology than just being a therapist. And that a psychiatrist was a medical doctor, which I knew I didn't want to be. Also, our class took a field trip to a state mental hospital, and that seemed like a really depressing place to work. I thought some of the research that social psychologists did was very interesting. For a while, I thought I might want to be a researcher, but I don't think I want to be in school that long."

"A lot of psychologists at the corporate level have PhDs," Dr. Score says. "And you pretty well have to have a Master's to get started. The doctorate isn't as rigid a requirement for industrial psychologists though as it is for clinicians or if you want to teach at the college level."

"That's encouraging. It's not that I don't like college. It's just that I'm not sure I could afford to go to graduate school for very many years. Dr. Schwartz is trying to start up a graduate co-op program, and that could help me finance a master's degree if that's what I wind up doing."

"I think that's an excellent idea, but go on with what you were saying."

Janet, who was nervous about imposing on Dr. Score, is starting to feel more comfortable. He seems genuinely interested in helping her. She settles back in the chair and continues.

"We all had to take career tests in high school. I had interests in common with psychologists and social workers, but I also scored fairly high in a lot of the business careers. I'm in Dr. Schwartz's Intro class, and he told me Industrial/Organizational Psych might be a way for me to combine my interests and get into a branch of psychology that has a lot of opportunities.

"I made good grades in high school, and I made two B's and two A's my first quarter in college. I made right at 600 on both parts of my SAT. I'm pretty sure I'm going to make an A in Psych 301 this quarter. I don't consider myself a nerd, but I'm not afraid to work hard on my studies. I hope that gives you some idea about me. Can you tell me about your work here at Acme and how you got into organizational psychology?"

Listen attentively as your contact describes the field under discussion and what it's like to work in it. But do more than just listen. Obviously, it would be inappropriate to interrupt, but it's good form to interact. If some aspect of your contact's job particularly interests you, say so. Ask her for more details or how she feels about it. When you ask intelligent questions in a confident manner, you not only learn more, you are viewed as intelligent as well. See suggested questions to ask on an informational interview at the end of this chapter.

As you finish your interview, ask your contact if she can suggest other people who could give you useful information. Depending upon where you are in your program, you may want to ask your contact to critique your resume. Say your thank-you, and follow it up with a letter of thanks. Look over Chapters 7 and 10 to get more ideas on interviewing and networking.

■ Career Planning Is a Process

Career planning is an ongoing process that unfolds throughout your lifetime. It's not a decision you make once and for all while you're in college. College is, however, an especially active time of deliberation about your career. You have to pick a major. You're beginning to narrow your focus down to broad themes. About half of all college students change their majors at least once. Investigating different courses of study is often a necessary step in self-discovery. The word "vocation" is derived from the Latin word for "calling."

Finding work that fits you, that enables you to express yourself, that will give you satisfaction throughout your life is one of college's major tasks. Because of the constancy of change in contemporary society young people are advised that they will probably have many jobs and several careers. I believe there is wisdom in this advice. I also believe that you'll be most productive and gain the most satisfaction when your many jobs and several careers are congruent with who you are. As you clarify for yourself your own vocational identify, it's also helpful to know that your career as opposed to your vocation will very probably undergo a variety of changes. Managing your career so as to provide opportunity and financial security while expressing your vocation or calling will be a considerable challenge in the 21st Century.

Students often ask us which careers have the most promise. The answer, of course, is that beyond the big brush strokes which the Information Age paints for all of us, no one knows for sure. The job market of the future depends on the interaction of the national and world economies, technological innovations, demographic changes, and various other factors. Here are some factors to consider.

■ The Job Market of the 21st Century

Working in the Knowledge Economy

If you buy the fact that knowledge is power in the Information Age, it's a "no-brainer" to conclude that higher education will be strongly correlated with professional and material success. Increasingly, a college degree is regarded as a minimum requirement, a union card without which your choices are severely limited. Even more important than a degree, however, is what the degree stands for: knowledge. Moreover, since knowledge is growing at an ever-accelerating rate, it is not possible to learn a big chunk of knowledge that will serve you throughout your lifetime. Being a learned person is less important than being a learning person. College is the time to cultivate an inquisitive mindset. It's the time to learn how to access information in libraries and on the Internet. The successful person in the 21st Century will be the one who commits to life-long learning.

Chaotic Career Paths

The secure, lifetime job is history. Very few of you who read this sentence will get a job out of college and stick with the same company for 30–40 years until you attend a retirement banquet and get your gold watch.

Let's take a look at some of the evidence for the death of the secure, lifetime job. For many years, IBM was regarded as one of the best run corporations in the world. IBM was worth more than the GNP of most countries in the world. IBM was noted for its loyalty to its employees, a loyalty which was highly reciprocal. Many IBMers counted on and prospered through life-long employment with Big Blue, as the company was called by friend and competitor alike.

In 1995, IBM was in a state of turmoil. For several years, thousands of its employees each year had been laid off, pushed into early retirement, or demoralized by a state of chronic job insecurity, wondering: Am I the next to go? Of course, IBM was not the only

There is a contrarian point of view that has some merit. It goes like this. The quality of American education has fallen so drastically that high school and college degrees don't mean much any more. What ensures success is not the number of degrees you have, but the number of skills you have mastered. While certain professions, such as medicine, will always require a specialized degree which attests to expertise, there will be many endeavors which will not. There are, for example, many computer jobs which are filled by people who have learned the necessary skills on their own. (Legions of self-taught hackers come to mind) or via OTJ (On-the-Job) training.

Some people think that eventually the notion of a four-year college degree will go the way of the horse and buggy. People will continue to go to college, but in more flexible ways. A person might take a few general courses, and then specialize in a discipline that provides a set of marketable skills. Some will stick around for months, some for years, depending on their particular career goals.

The point to bear in mind here is that knowledge is the source of power. Whether you get it in or out of a formal setting, you're dead in the water without it.

corporation which struggled. AT&T, General Motors, Delta, as well as many smaller companies downsized, right-sized, and got lean and mean. IBM has for the time being righted itself. It now has, however, fewer full-time employees. And those employees are not accorded lifetime job security. Nor has the practice of corporate reorganization stopped. In January of 2000, Coke International announced that it was cutting some 8,000 jobs.

According to Alvin Toffler, the principal reason for all the chaos is because we are in a state of transition from the Industrial Age to the Information Age. That's certainly a part of it.

Another reason is because of the globalization of the world economy. (There would, of course, be no global economy were there no Information Age.) General Motors competes with Toyota and Honda as well as Ford and Chrysler. And Chrysler is now Daimler-Chrysler. Ford includes Volvo. IBM competes with NEC as well as Dell and Apple. US Steel must do battle with steel manufacturers in Japan, Korea, and Brazil as well as with other American companies. That means American companies must cut out any and all fat. Sometimes, muscle and bone are lost in the process.

Another factor is the outsourcing of many of our labor needs. It's cheaper to hire assembly line workers in Mexico than Michigan. It costs less to hire clerks to process insurance claims in Ireland than in Illinois. And if you don't aspire to a career as a clerk or instrument assembler, Motorola sends problems by satellite to India where engineers and computer scientists, often American educated, are paid a fraction of what their American counterparts earn.

As competition, outsourcing of jobs, and automation tighten the screws on the job market, your problem will be: how can you manage your career? More immediately, what can you start doing now, while you're in college, to shore up your future?

And if you're still skeptical about our argument, please read what Dr. Howard Figler has to say in the February 1995 Career Planning and Adult Development Network Newsletter.

More important than missing out on the gold watch is lacking a viable pension plan. We will not elaborate on this issue now. After all, you're probably just a freshman. We will tell you that your first step after graduation should not be to purchase an expensive car; it should be to start a financial plan that you will invest in throughout your life.

Know How to Market Yourself

Since the secure, lifetime job with a giant corporation is a relic of a bygone era, you will have to persuade many different clients many different times to buy your services. If you don't know who you are and what you have to offer, you won't have many customers. Managing your career entrepreneurially is frustrating, anxious-making, and a threat to your security. Entrepreneurial career management is also invigorating, challenging, and the wave of the future.

A Return to the Real America

For the past 50 years "regular employment" has been so much the norm that American free enterprise has gotten lost in the shuffle. That 50-year historical blip is over. In its place, people are learning to be more enterprising, to regard themselves as self-employed. Dan Lacey predicted the fading of steady jobs in The Paycheck Disruption, *and Cliff Hakim's new book,* We Are All Self-Employed, *tells us how to re-orient ourselves as career seekers. Waterman, Waterman, and Collard's 1994 article in the* Harvard Business Review *guides employers in understanding the big picture.*

Free enterprise is making a comeback. Increasingly, present or former wage-earners are taking on the self-employment attitude by doing two things: (1) Giving stronger consideration to business ownership as a possible career, as either a primary or supplementary form of income, (2) Adopting an enterprise-oriented attitude even when they are employed by someone else. If you worked for someone, have the perspective that it's YOUR company, your money, and your reputation. You will see your job with a new pair of glasses.

It's teeth-grinding time in the US of A. With fewer steady jobs and more contingency workers, people wonder how they will make it. There's no escaping the answer—those who embrace the free enterprise attitude will survive and prosper.

Entrepreneuring is woven into the fabric of this country, but we are oblivious to this because steady employment ruled during all of our working lifetimes. You can get some perspective on this by listening to what Abraham Lincoln had to say about career development:

> "The prudent, penniless beginner in the world labors for wages a while, saves a surplus with which to buy tools or land . . .; then labors on his own account for a while, and at length hires another new beginner to help him. This is the just and generous, and prosperous system, which opens the way to all, gives hope to all."

Lincoln's words remind us that self-employment and business ownership are the ways of our country. Employment is only a temporary condition; ownership is the long-term goal. According to Lincoln, it's moral, prudent, and it makes good sense to have control over your economic life.

John Hancock said that not only is ownership good for you, it's good for the nation:

> "The more people who own little businesses of their own, the safer our country will be . . . for the people who have stake in their country and their community are its best citizens."

Look at it this way—even if you get a salary check each week, the company is only renting your skills, and who knows how long they will want you? As Bill Bridges, has said, we are all temporary workers, but 80% of us are in denial.

The ground has been tilled for a new entrepreneurial era in America. Those who see themselves as self-marketers will prosper. Those who cling to the idea that job performance will sustain them will become victims of market forces. Let me give you an example. Neil "did his job" as a travel agent for several years until the agency lost its customer base and closed its doors. He had seen the service slipping badly. Tour bookings decreased as the staff lost its enthusiasm. Customer records were lost. Neil watched in dismay but said little, fearing that he would "rock the boat." "Not my job" became a prelude to disaster. Neil has since joined an agency where he speaks up regularly about business, and is building his capital to buy a stake in the ownership.

The Information Era makes it possible for many people to be self-employed without a large capital investment. Self-employment is an attitude. You have a set of skills and areas of knowledge. You put these to use where they will do the most good and yield the most gain. Your customers (which includes your employers) decide how your skills fit their needs, and money changes hands. In between your skills and their need is the fine art of selling. We all sell continually, we just don't call it that.

America was never meant to be a country where people indentured themselves to companies and called this "lifetime employment." Yes, you may do it temporarily, but you have greater freedom when you view yourself as being in charge.

Career counselors will spend a lot of their time helping people to grab hold of self-employment and free enterprise as concepts, because most are not ready for it. We have been parented by large organizations for a long time. Many will long for the good old days. But, of course, assisting people with their difficult career transitions is what we're here for—to help clients adapt to the reemergence of American enterprise rather than hide from it.

Dr. Gene Griessman, who wrote *The Achievement Factors*, recommends that every college student should take a course in sales. You can't sell yourself to a prospective employer if you don't know who you are and what you have to offer. You can have a satisfying career, but it's not going to happen by accident. It takes a hard, honest look at yourself and an active search of the job world.

Acquire Computer Literacy

Computer literacy will be virtually essential at work and at home—which will increasingly be one and the same. Accountants will keep their books on computer files. Architects and illustrators will do much of their designing on computers. Managers will make many of their decisions with the aid of a computer spreadsheet. People in sales will show their wares on laptops which play multimedia. Pretty much everybody will write with word processing, correspond with e-mail, and receive information via the Internet. E-commerce will increasingly be the way business is done. Computers will grow cheaper, smaller, more powerful, and more user-friendly. Unless you're specializing in hardware or software, you won't need to know computer languages. For the foreseeable future, however, your life will be a lot easier if you can type well using the touch system. You will have to be comfortable with a seemingly endless supply of new applications if you want to stay current. John Naisbitt, chronicler of megatrends, compares computer illiteracy today with wandering around an enormous library in which all the books are randomly arranged. All that information, and no way to use it.

Global Economy Requires Global Communication Skills

In 1985, I surveyed corporate recruiters regarding the importance of knowing additional languages. "Not very," is what they told us. Fifteen years later, companies often expect facility with more than English. Having command of an "exotic" language such as Chinese, Japanese, or Arabic can be even more attractive. A safe bet is certainly Spanish. Probably even more important than knowing other languages is familiarity with other cultures. We recently heard a management consultant tell an auditorium full of freshmen that virtually all of them would work outside of the continental United States within their lifetimes. Also, we were talking recently with an economics student back from a

What do you call a person who knows three languages? Trilingual.

What do you call a person who knows two languages? Bilingual.

What do you call a person who knows just one language? American!

Don't be an "ugly American!"

year's internship in Japan. The student was convinced that the biggest barrier to increasing our exports to Japan was the simple fact that American products did not have clear Japanese instructions on them. He added that it was typical for American corporate representatives to show up at a Japanese trade show without even a rudimentary knowledge of the Japanese language and culture. This puts American businessmen at a tremendous disadvantage with their Japanese counterparts, most of whom do speak English. Small wonder there's a trade imbalance.

The Rand Institute reported in 1994 that most colleges do NOT do a good job of preparing their graduates for the global economy. Language departments frequently focus on classical literature and devote no attention to the ability to read a foreign newspaper. Conversational skills often suffer at the expense of reading and writing. The absolute best way to study a language is to immerse yourself in it. Living in a language house will force you to speak that language. A language house is a residence hall in which the residents commit to speaking only that language—say French—within the hall.

Another excellent strategy is study abroad. The most effective study abroad programs have you studying, working, playing with students, colleagues, and families from the host country. The great thing about this approach is you are immersed in the culture as well as the language. But this means you need to know the language really well before you go. And this means you need to choose a language house early on in your college career.

We highly recommend the language house/study abroad sequence as the ideal way to prepare for the global economy. There are other, less challenging, methods that everyone can take advantage of. Most American colleges and universities have international students and faculty. Spend time with them. Get to know them. You probably can join the International Students Association through which you can rub elbows with a variety of cultures. Catch some foreign films. Attend some cultural events which showcase international talent. The bottom line is really cross cultural sensitivity. Don't fail to meet the bottom line.

Learn To Relate

We've already told you that the success stories in the 21st Century will have an entrepreneurial flair. Effective entrepreneurs know how to market themselves. No matter how competent you are, you still have to convince others to buy your services. That entails some self-assurance and some self-understanding—not always in ready supply for a 20-something, much less for someone 18 or 19. The best thing we can tell you is that with practice you can get better, but that is only IF you practice. You get practice through involvement—co-op jobs, internships, campus organizations, and activities (See Chapter 6.).

Another aspect of entrepreneurial career planning is leadership. Entrepreneurs are "in charge." If you're in charge of your career you must have a vision of where you're headed and what you want to accomplish. You must have enough desire to persevere

The prospect of being a leader may seem daunting, but leadership is comprised of a constellation of skills that you can develop.

in the face of obstacles and hardships. You need the ability to convince others that the pursuit of your goal is good for them as well. The prospect of being a leader may seem daunting, but leadership is comprised of a constellation of skills that you can develop. (See Chapters 15.)

Get Organized

Organizational skills are useful for just about anybody who wants to accomplish anything. Systematic study produces better learning and higher grades than random chaos does. Attention to detail (which, I confess, is hardly my long suit) makes any job run more smoothly. In this section, however, we are specifically talking about organizing your career planning. Entrepreneurs set goals, develop strategies for reaching them, and then organize their efforts. Since we believe career planning in the 21st Century will have an entrepreneurial flavor, you must organize your career planning. If you're smart, you won't wait until you're a senior to start.

What to organize:

1. Contacts. Keep a file, Rolodex™, or electronic data base of people that can help you succeed. As a freshman, you'll probably want tutors, study buddies, professors, counselors, and advisors on this list. As you progress in college, you should add the names of career related contacts. We recommend anyone you've met at a career fair, people you've interviewed for career information, co-op advisors, and people who have supervised your work.
2. Resume. Maintain a resume on a computer disk. Keep it updated as you acquire new experiences and develop new skills.
3. Portfolio. Keep a folder that contains any awards, letters of recommendation, news clippings, and evaluations. Keep any outstanding work samples. This may seem formidable for a freshman, but as you continue your education, school work such as senior design projects and term papers can be included. If you've been an intern for a newspaper, you would naturally want to keep clippings of any articles you wrote. If you volunteered at a hospital, you'd want to keep the brochure describing the services your department offered.
4. Career Information. Keep a file of pertinent articles and reports on job trends and job search strategies.

Plan for the Future

Cultivate "the art of the long view," which happens to be the title of a book by futurist Peter Schwartz. Most of us don't have the time to do the exhaustive research that Schwartz and other futurists like Toffler, and Naisbitt conduct, but you can read what they have written. It makes sense to think about the future and how it will affect your life and impact your career. Read trade journals, *The Occupational Outlook Handbook,* and thoughtful news analyses and commentaries. In other words, expand your horizons beyond *People Magazine, TV Guide,* and your required textbooks.

How, then, do you plan your career in the Information Age? You do so entrepreneurially. That means you're in charge, but you can't navigate without information about yourself and the job world. You must be aggressive, intellectually curious, proactive, and honest with yourself. You should strive for self understanding and keep your eyes peeled for information about the world outside yourself. While it is important to read "career information," it is equally important to stay informed in a broader sense. When you come to think about it, what isn't career information in the world of tomorrow? Watch the news, look at the business section in the newspaper, and keep up with science and technology.

■ What if I'm Still not Sure?

We're not surprised if you're a little uncertain. Life is filled with uncertainties. Some of you will be working twenty years from now in fields that haven't even been invented yet. If you want a 100 percent guarantee, you might consider inherited wealth. If you can't work that one out, and most of us can't, here are some other guidelines:

1. *Money isn't everything.* Sure, it's important, and you'd be a fool to ignore your future financial security. But we're tired of talking to pre-meds who are more concerned with BMW's than Biochemistry. With engineering students who can't stand math and science, but figure they're going to ride the high-tech wave to megabucks. *Don't sentence yourself to a lifetime of work you're going to hate.*

   A generation of psychological research on the workplace has found that people were most satisfied when they were doing what they really wanted to do. Research by Teresa Amabile of Brandeis suggests that they are most creative as well. After a certain level of income, salary and pats on the back have only a negligible impact on performance.

   Besides, career choices are seldom limited to being a starving artist in Soho or a well-heeled financier on Wall Street. Why not be a creative director on Madison Avenue?

2. *There is no magic timetable.* Not even our Four-Year Master Plan. We're convinced it's a good general guide, but divine revelation it isn't. You don't *have* to declare a major by your sophomore year. And there's no crime in changing majors. The main thing is *don't just sit on your hands when it comes to choosing a major and planning your career.* Do the exercises and follow the suggestions in this chapter. Don't wander passively through college.

3. *There is no perfect career.* Nor does everyone "fall in love" with a career. True, some people are born doctors or lawyers or managers, but most aren't. Don't expect to hear angelic choirs every time you tackle a calculus problem just because you're majoring in physics.

   There might be a dozen jobs out there that could meet your needs. Don't get tunnel vision and insist on one occupation and no other. What if you don't get into medical school? Or a good MBA program? Make sure you've got some decent alternatives in mind if everything doesn't go just as you planned it. Even the most successful people have their setbacks. You'll have many jobs throughout your professional life. And most of you will have more than one career.

■ Summary

1. You're going to spend much of your adult life at work. Find a field that fits you.
2. Conscientiously assess your interests, abilities, and needs.
3. Thoroughly investigate relevant majors and careers. Stay abreast of current events and try to anticipate future trends.
4. Participate in student professional societies. Periodically, look over trade journals in fields of interest.
5. Go to the source. Interview people who actually do the work you think you might like.
6. Get help planning your career from whatever professional resources are available on your campus.

7. Getting career-related work before you graduate is one of the best ways to test your career choice.

8. Learn a second language. Acquire cross-cultural sensitivity.

9. No one can predict precisely what the future job world will be like. Therefore, general skills such as the ability to communicate, computer literacy, and the capacity to learn new information are keys to future career success.

10. Organize your career planning effort.

■ Career Planning Checklist

The following list of steps is arranged in approximately chronological order. How many have you already completed? (Mark with a 1.) How many have you not yet completed, but have scheduled to do in your planner? (Mark with a 2.) How many will you have completed before you graduate? (Mark with a 3.)

_____ 1. I understand my interests and abilities pretty well.

_____ 2. I can see that my interests and abilities fit with my major.

_____ 3. I have a good idea of the classes I have to take to complete my degree.

_____ 4. I have a good understanding of the daily activities that exist in my chosen field and the typical career paths that practitioners follow.

_____ 5. I have discussed my major at length with a professor.

_____ 6. I have interviewed someone in the field I plan to enter.

_____ 7. I have a high quality resume saved on my computer.

_____ 8. I can give a good oral resume.

_____ 9. I've had my resume critiqued by a professional.

_____ 10. I know how the interview process works and could effectively answer a job interviewer's typical questions.

_____ 11. I have attended a meeting of the professional society associated with my field.

_____ 12. I am a member of the professional society associated with my field.

_____ 13. I have career-related work experience.

_____ 14. I have read a trade journal in my chosen field.

_____ 15. I regularly read a trade journal in my chosen field.

_____ 16. I have attended a professional society national convention.

_____ 17. I have at least three contacts from my field.

_____ 18. I know at least one professor who would write me a strong recommendation.

_____ 19. I know whether graduate or professional school is required for my career.

_____ 20. I know which graduate or professional schools are a good match for me.

(Whether you're choosing a major, changing majors, or changing careers, the above steps are useful to take.)

CHAPTER 6
Beyond the Classroom
Learning Through Experience

While academic excellence is an important ingredient in building success, it is by no means the only one. If you really want to build a successful life, you will seize some of the many opportunities outside of the classroom. Some will be on campus, some will be in the community, and some will be in the workplace. If knowledge is the coin of the realm in the Information Age and managing your career is an entrepreneurial adventure, then the time to dive in is now.

■ Campus Involvement

The job world you will face throughout your career will be fluid and dynamic. In fact, it will be downright chaotic. For that reason, the people skills that make for successful entrepreneurs will be required of everyone. You will have to manage, lead, follow, persuade, sell, network, collaborate, delegate, and coach with countless people in numerous ways.

One of the best ways to cultivate the multi-dimensional talents the 21st century will demand of you is through your involvement in organizations. A recent survey conducted by AT&T indicated that participation in extracurricular activities was an excellent predictor of managerial potential. So, come job-hunting time, expect to be asked about what you did outside the classroom. If you did nothing, how will you explain this fact? Did you join several organizations, but only to pad your resume? A good interviewer will find out whether you were really involved or not. Did you hold an office? What were your duties? On which committees did you serve? What did you accomplish?

Rather than looking at campus involvement as more fodder for your resume, we recommend that you look at extracurricular activities as opportunities for personal development. Do you want to be an executive someday? Then lead a group or head up some project. Do you want to have a network of professional contacts? Then a good place to begin is through a student professional association. Through the right group you can also learn about different kinds of people and get some exposure to new ideas.

We recommend that early on in your college career you identify one weakness or missing skill and try to develop it through some extracurricular activity. Do not, however, forget fun. You'll go nuts if you do nothing but chase success. What's the point of being successful if you never get any pleasure out of life? Besides, we are social animals. It is not likely that you will ever have a better opportunity for developing close, possibly lifelong friends than while you are in college. One of the best ways to meet people is through clubs and activities.

Most colleges and universities have a wide array of organizations from which to choose. At Georgia Tech, there are approximately 300! While they cover a broad range of interests, they can more or less be broken into nine categories:

- Department/Professional Societies (Society of Chemical Engineers, Entrepreneurs Club)
- Social organizations (Fraternities and Sororities)
- Honor Societies (Phi Beta Kappa, Golden Key)
- Production Organizations (School newspaper, literary magazine, radio station)
- Student Governing Organizations (Panhellenic, Student Government, Hall Councils)

- ■ Recreation/Leisure (Chess Club, Outdoor Recreation, Parachute Club)
- ■ Religious and Spiritual Organizations (Baptist Student Union, Muslim Student Association)
- ■ Service and Education Organizations (Habitat for Humanity, Toastmasters)
- ■ Cultural and Diversity (Arab Student Association, African American Student Union)

While some of these clubs are mostly for fun and others are mostly business, you can develop a number of skills that you'll use throughout your professional life: leadership, communication, persuasion, administration, negotiation. You learn through experience how things get done in an organization.

Do you want to establish a student course critique on your campus? It will take time and energy. You'll have to rally student, faculty, and administrative support in order to get the idea accepted. Compromises will have to be made. And once the legislation is passed, there's the not-so-small matter of implementation. Who develops the surveys? Who decides on the final format? How are they administered and scored? Who writes up the critique? How is it distributed? And how is the whole project funded?

By involving yourself in a project of this magnitude, you can learn things you just don't usually learn in a classroom. And, yes, it does look good on your resume and sound good during an interview.

■ Getting Started

Get a list of campus organizations from the office of the Dean of Students or from the Web site which provides such information. Ask around. What organizations provide the best laboratories for leadership development, professional development, making contacts? Attend the meetings of some organizations. Talk with officers and members. Get a feel for the activities and "culture" of the club. If the group appeals to you, come back for more. If it still looks good, join. Be wary of overextending, especially as a freshman. Once you're convinced a club is for you, deepen your involvement. Serve on a committee. Help organize a project. You're on your way.

■ Career-Related Work: Don't Leave School Without It

We believe higher education is one of the most important investments you can make in preparing for the next century. Do not, however, make the mistake of avoiding the "real world" while you're in school. In particular, don't avoid the world of work. This has always been true, but real world experience will be more important than ever in the highly fluid world of work that lies ahead. We've said that the future belongs to the learners and the entrepreneurs. A successful entrepreneur is constantly upgrading skills, learning about the competition, guestimating about the future. That's the attitude you need in the classroom AND the workplace.

It's better to design software at MicroSoft than to bus tables in a microbrewery. It's also better to manage a waitstaff for a microbrewery than to push a broom at MicroSoft. But any work is better than none at all. Working teaches you the importance of effort—employers appreciate and reward hard workers. Do you have to work part-time to put yourself through school? A lot of students do. It can be stressful, but you learn how to be self-sufficient. You also learn how to budget your time—you have no choice if you want to keep your grades respectable. Working teaches you responsibility, how to get along with all kinds of people.

Work experience makes you more marketable. Employers like it when candidates have worked their way through school. We urge graduating seniors to highlight this fact on their resumes, even if they contributed only a portion of what their education cost them. But career-related work is even better. What you learn is more relevant to your future, a fact that won't be overlooked by prospective employers when you graduate.

The right jobs while you're still in school will teach you about professional work. Co-ops and interns often work for corporations. They learn about a large company's different divisions. A nurse's aide might learn what it's like to work in a hospital or clinic. Even a file clerk can get a feel for how an office really operates. There will also be opportunities to make contacts—people who can write recommendations for you, give you leads for jobs, perhaps someday hire you for an important position.

One of the most valuable lessons you will learn is just where you fit into your chosen field. Or if you fit into it. Most college students change majors at least once. Better to find out as a rising sophomore than as a senior.

We emphasize the importance of career goals throughout this book. But that doesn't mean that all students settle on a career by the beginning of their second semester and, after that, it's smooth sailing. In fact, we believe choosing a career is a lifelong process. When you work summers in a law office, you get a first-hand feel for what the legal profession is like. This is much more valid experience than you'll get from watching reruns of *L.A. Law.* Developing a career means continually trying on roles to see how suitable they are to your interests and abilities. Do I like doing this? Can I do it well? And is there a future in it?

 Part-time and summer work that is career-related helps you to refine your goals.

Part-time and summer work that is career-related also helps you to refine your goals. Suppose you've known since high school that you wanted to work in a scientific/technical field. After some research you think that civil engineering might be for you. But which branch? Construction? Sewage disposal? Roads and bridges? Urban planning? Working in one or more of these areas can help you decide. And the sooner you get the experience, the sooner you'll know if it's right for you.

Career-related work enhances your academic experience. Sometimes it's difficult to see just how the theories in your textbooks can be put into practice. There can be a big gap between the ivory-tower atmosphere of school and the real-world problems encountered on the job. By working in your field of interest before you graduate, you can start to apply some of what you've learned in the classroom. And when you get back to school, many of your subjects become more relevant. You'll also have a better idea of what advanced electives to take.

Many colleges and universities have a cooperative education plan. Georgia Tech's program has been in place since 1912. Over 3,000 students participate in the plan each year. Tech co-ops are almost twice as likely to make the Dean's List as are students who aren't in the co-op program. Their work helps to make them better students.

One of the most valuable aspects of career-related work before you graduate is that you begin to develop the very skills and expertise that you will practice after you receive your degree. Do you want to make big bucks some day in sales? There's no better way to learn about selling than to start knocking on doors. Do you want to inspire a curiosity for learning in primary school children? Practice teaching will probably be your most useful experience. But don't wait until you're a senior to get a taste of it—find a job at a summer camp, a girls' club, or the YMCA. Do you want to be a plant manager? Try your hand on a production line for a while.

Many college students aspire to managerial positions someday. The sooner you get some supervisory experience, the better. A highly successful business consultant wryly related his son's first experience as a hotel management intern. The son had anticipated starting out behind the checkout counter. Instead, he was placed in charge of the cleanup crew in the main kitchen. He had to manage sixteen older, ethnically different, relatively uneducated men. It was a stressful internship for the student, but he learned a lot about people. He had some very challenging questions to pose to his management profs when he returned to school. And he was a much stronger job candidate after he graduated.

■ Be a Student Entrepreneur

We find that many college students want to own their own businesses someday. Well, you don't have to wait until you've save up $50,000 seed money. You can start while you're still in school. In fact, there are students who establish flourishing enterprises even before they graduate.

Even if you don't plan on starting your own business in the future, starting a small one now can be an excellent way to develop new skills. The smallest undertaking can be a learning laboratory. In order to make a business go, you've got to come up with an idea and make that idea come to life. You've got to analyze the market, develop your products or services, market them, handle finances and accounting. If other people are involved, there are personnel questions to handle. And, of course, you've got to deal with your customers. Plus it's all *your* responsibility.

That sort of experience is music to an employer's ears. In many instances you can get academic credit for a business venture. And you can pick up some spare change, in some instances quite a lot of it. Mark McKee was the president of two companies by the end of his junior year at the University of Kansas. Pyramid Pizza earned $700,000 that year. Waddles Active Wear, which specializes in Hawaiian clothes, grossed $2 million. In 1986 Louis Kahn of Atlanta owned and operated a worldwide computer network, a computer mail-order catalog, a service for real-estate brokers, a small book publishing company, and an in-house ad agency. He was about to graduate from high school. Michael Dell started his computer company while he was a student at the University of Texas at Austin. I'm writing this chapter on a Dell computer, so I'm guessing he did something right. Dennis Hayes invented the modem while he was a student at Georgia Tech. Recently, Kris Claus developed some software to enhance computer security while he was a student at Georgia Tech. He started selling it. His business grew so rapidly that he had to hire others to keep up with the demand. Eventually, he hired an experienced manager with an MBA. A couple of years later he went public. He's now worth well over $100 million dollars and still on the sunny side of thirty.

How do you get started? There is no one way, but students have made a go of all kinds of businesses including delivering munchies to dorm rooms, bumper stickers, t-shirts with messages, flower delivery, grocery delivery, tutoring, computer repair, computer consultant. The possibilities are limited only by your imagination and drive.

Some years ago, Larry Adler started by doing magic shows at kids' birthday parties. Then he started selling baskets full of favors at the same parties. Then he began distributing the baskets to retail stores. He phoned around to find better favors for his baskets. He was so impressed with one item that he asked if he could represent the company that manufactured it. He was told they already had a sales rep in the area where he lived. Could he be their sub-rep? Well, what would it hurt? Go ahead and try. His first month he won a set of matched luggage for being a sales leader. No one else in sales had ever been a leader for that company during their first month. After that he represented a number of companies that marketed children's products. A reporter asked how he did it. Larry said he was successful because he knew what kids would buy. He probably did—he was twelve years old when he was interviewed.

For the mortals among you, consider first taking a course in entrepreneurship. Many universities offer them now. Join the Entrepreneur's Club on your campus. Read popular magazines such as *Enterprise* or *INC*. Talk with other student entrepreneurs. Talk with your professors. The main thing, however, is to come up with some ideas and put them into action. Additionally, there are many resources on the internet. Here are a few:

Helpful Websites:

Georgia Tech Entrepreneur Club
www.cyberbuzz.gatech.edu/eclub

National Foundation for Women Business Owners
www.nfwbo.org
email—NFWBO@worldnet.att.net
1100 Wayne Ave., Suite 830
Silver Spring, MD 20910-5603
Phone—(301)495-4975
FAX—(301)495-4979

Success on the Web—a free business education on the Web
www.success.org

Better Business Bureau
Atlanta Bureau: PO Box 2707, Atlanta, GA 30301
Phone—(404)688-4910

Collegiate Entrepreneurs Organization—dues are $15
www.c-e-o.org
Institute for Entrepreneurial Studies MC 244
601 South Morgan St., Suite 809
Chicago, IL 60607-7108
Phone: (312)996-2670 or (312)996-2608

◾ How To Get a Good Job while You're Still a Student

It might seem like a tall order to find career-related employment when you're only eighteen or nineteen, but it can be done. Remember Larry Adler. Your school's co-operative plan or internship program is probably the path of least resistance, and we recommend both to you.

Co-op plans usually arrange ongoing, paid work alternating with school throughout a student's stay in college. By the time students are in their last semester of work, they usually make pretty good money. By that time they earn it, because they will have developed the skills that enable them to perform relatively sophisticated tasks.

Internships are more often one-time arrangements. Although many provide salaries, some offer only experience. If it's the right experience, it may still be invaluable. You know the old dilemma: you can't get a job without experience, but you can't get experience without a job. An internship may be your solution to the dilemma.

Internships also tend to draw less technically skilled students than do co-op plans. They provide an opportunity for someone to get a first exposure to a field, to try it on for size.

Even without the assistance of a formal program, you should be able to find some sort of job. In fact, landing a good job on your own is an impressive accomplishment and will be noted as such by future employers. Finding a job is a job in itself, and mastering the art of getting hired is a skill that you will use repeatedly throughout your life. When I wrote the book that preceded this one, I reported that college graduates would change jobs an average of eight times before they retired. In the 21st Century, you may change CAREERS eight times.

Read Chapters 10–12 which discuss the different phases of the job search. Pay special attention to "Resumes While Still In School" in Chapter 11 and "Questions Asked of Co-ops" in Chapter 12. The sort of job you can get depends a lot on how many skills you have already developed. But suppose you haven't developed many as yet. You're full of potential, but without much actual experience or expertise.

Don't give up. It simply means that you're going to have to start at the bottom (better now than after graduation). Your first job may be as a gofer (go fer this, and then go fer that). But if you perform your menial duties enthusiastically and look for opportunities, you should be able gradually to assume some larger responsibilities. The idea is eventually to work yourself into a position that offers more challenge and fosters more professional growth.

In some cases you can earn academic credit along with your salary while you work. Sometimes you can get only one or the other. We recommend that you attempt to arrange some kind of credit. If there's no formal internship program on your campus, see what you can work out with your professors as an independent study. We heard of one student who got academic credit while working as cashier in a convenience store. She observed that different types of people used the store at different hours of the day. She recorded her observations systematically and eventually turned them into a sociology report.

■ What to Look for in a First Job

There are three things to consider—experience, experience, and experience. Naturally money is nice too. If you're working your way through college it's a necessity, but you usually won't be paid well without experience. Conversely, if you are paid well, it's probably because you're performing some important tasks for your employer. In other words, you're getting good experience.

Joan Macal, while president of the Board of Directors of the National Society for Internships and Experiential Education, recommended the following guidelines for interns:

- Secure a written learning contract. What are your duties? What will you learn?
- Try to secure regular meetings with supervisors from both work and school.
- Request a written evaluation of your performance and learning.

■ Learning about Life: Learning for Life

You are entering an era in which change is rapid and constant, and knowledge is power. Learning is not confined to the classroom. It's an ongoing, lifelong process. The world is your classroom, and you're in charge of learning as much as possible.

One of the hot new trends in the business community today is the "learning organization." Successful organizations hire eager learners, support their continuing education, and provide an atmosphere in which ideas are exchanged, skills are shared, and learning is pervasive. EDS, the software giant founded by Ross Perot is one such organization. Every EDS site has a bulletin board on which staffers post what they've been reading. Books and articles are exchanged. Ideas are discussed. An employee says that's one of the most exciting things about working for EDS. There is a culture of learning, and it's infectious. Since lifelong learning is the only way to survive in the next century, she figures working for EDS is better than unemployment insurance.

An executive recently informed a room full of MBA students that his corporation expects employees to chart their own professional development. The corporation will pay for just about any workshop or class, but it's up to the individual to find the right class, attend it, and get the most out of it. Many employees never get around to doing so. They will be the most vulnerable to downsizing.

While it's great to work for a learning organization, you must first become a learning individual. There is no job, no class, no activity from which you can't learn something. All you need is an inquisitive mind.

In conclusion, and at the risk of belaboring the point, get some career-related work experience. It is one of the very best ways you can invest in your own future.

■ Summary

1. Don't limit your education to the classroom.
2. Get involved, but don't spread yourself too thin.
3. You can build your success by building skills through organizational involvement.
4. By building your leadership skills, you can significantly build your ability to succeed.
5. Make contacts and close friends.
6. Learn about your career through professional societies.
7. Enjoy yourself and have a good time.
8. Employers value work experience, especially if it's career related.
9. Career-related experience helps you discover whether or not your chosen field suits you.
10. Career-related experience teaches you about the world of work you'll enter upon graduation.
11. Career-related experience helps you to refine your professional goals.
12. Career-related work enhances your academic experience.
13. Career-related work enables you to develop the professional skills you will use after graduation.
14. Becoming a student entrepreneur is an excellent way to get experience.
15. Co-op plans and internships provide excellent opportunities for students to get their first career-related experience.

CHAPTER 7
Building Contacts to Build Success

You will see in the next chapter that high achievers are quick to get help from others. This chapter is about how you can build a network of contacts from whom you can get that help. Networking may seem like an activity suitable only for older professionals, but you can never start too soon. Moreover, networking can start paying dividends your freshman year. Getting someone to loan you a car, getting class notes for the day you were sick, finding a ride home for Thanksgiving, finding out where the best party will be this weekend, identifying the best calculus professor, knowing which tutor is most effective—all these problems are typically solved with the help of other people. As you rise in academic standing, the problems you will want to solve become more challenging: Where can I get a good internship? Which campus organizations provide the greatest opportunities for leadership development? Which professor can I get to speak to my organization? Who can I use as references to get a job or entrance into a top graduate school? By the time the savvy student nears graduation, (s)he will have dozens of friends, allies, professors, and knowledgeable professionals to call on for a variety of reasons: job leads, recommendations, information, collaboration, advice, support, and probably a dozen other things.

When do you start? A couple of years ago is ideal, but if that's not an option, then the best time is NOW! We often get resistance on this point along several lines.

Why would important people want to bother with me? Because it comes with the territory. Experts and people in power expect requests for information and assistance. Because most successful people want to help you succeed. This is especially true if they're convinced you're seriously committed to success. Because you make it worth their while. Life is give and take. If you help others, they'll usually help you. And if you're wondering what on earth you can do to help an older, established professional, we'll tell you later on in this chapter.

Isn't it insincere or maybe even downright manipulative to cultivate relationships for the sole purpose of advancing your career? Not at all. Most business relationships are just that—relationships that exist for the mutual benefit of both parties. Naturally, it's nicer if friendship develops as well, but it's not necessary. One word of warning, however, don't settle for having only a network of contacts. You need friends as well—people who accept you for who you are and not just what you can do for them.

Won't it detract from my success if I get help from others? Don't kid yourself. You can use a helping hand. We all can. This doesn't mean you get people to do for you what you can just as easily do for yourself.

But, as you'll see in Chapter 9, achievers take advantage of every resource in their environment. They actively seek out other people who can help them reach their goals. Don't waste ten years reinventing the wheel when you can buy tires at any service station in town.

But what if I'm shy? I have a hard enough time asking my roommate if I can borrow a computer disk. How am I going to ask some big shot to take time out of his or her busy schedule for me? Shyness can be a big obstacle to your success, so we urge you to take steps to overcome it. Use your campus resources: attend an assertiveness training workshop, take a speech class, get some counseling. In general, you can develop self-confidence by taking a series of small, gradually more difficult steps: next time ask your roommate for two computer disks!

Forward thinking students will develop a network of contacts:

1. Experts who can provide information or assistance;
2 Successful professionals who can advise you on your career path;
3. Persons in power who can open doors and give you job leads;
4. Mentors who can do a little of all three plus provide general support as well.

■ Information and Assistance

One of the best ways to learn about a field or a particular profession is to talk with experts who are leaders in that area. A description of how to go about doing that may be found in Chapter 5. It's a good idea to keep track of such people by entering them in your address book. There is probably a section of your planner which is suitable for recording such information. Some students prefer storing such information on their computer. Just remember that hard drives do crash, so be sure and back up such a database on a floppy disk. I have found that my organizational tools have a big impact on what I keep track of. Therefore, I suggest that you get an index-card or business-card file box for your office. (Students can have offices too, even if they consist only of a well-organized desk in a dormitory room.) Once you have accumulated a significant number of contacts, it's helpful to keep a little information about each person—the dates when you talked and what you talked about, the person's position or title, and what organization the person is affiliated with.

Experts can be business leaders or professors. They may be other students. They can be friends of your family or members of your church, temple, or mosque. You may need information about a prospective career, about a topic for a term paper, or the best place to stay at Ft. Lauderdale over spring break. The important thing is they have the information you need.

Helpful people can also provide assistance; how to solve a physics problem, a loan to tide you over for the last couple weeks of a school term, the key resource book you need to write your term paper. They can be a part of your overall support system.

■ Career Advice

We may be splitting hairs here, but we think advice is more complex and personal than mere information. Experienced professionals can do more than tell you the facts of their field. They can use their wisdom and experience to guide and advise you on your career journey. This doesn't mean you're obliged to follow every suggestion, but you should consider what a seasoned professional has to say. "Study Abroad: don't leave college without it." "Join Toastmasters. It will pay off more than you can imagine." "Consider starting out in sales, especially if you DON'T plan a career in that area." As you can see, each of these pieces of advice is more than information. These veterans are sharing of themselves, basing their advice on their experience in the school of hard knocks.

■ Job Leads

As you will see in Chapter 12, contacts can tell you where the jobs are. This includes "permanent" positions with a company or the time-limited projects which are more likely to be the norm in the 21st Century. Our research suggests that truly permanent jobs are going to be rare. Most career experts believe that contacts already are the best way to find a good job—"permanent" or project. Of course, it is important that you build your network of contacts all along the way so that you can call on them when it's time to look for a job.

■ Opening Doors

Experts are frequently in positions of power, and it is a huge plus to have powerful people on your side. If it's nice to get a lead on a good job, it's even nicer when someone with clout will recommend you highly for that job. And it's nicer still when such a person actually hires you. Similarly, it's a great help when someone can pave the way for a loan to start up your small business. And it's best of all when that person himself will agree to be your financial backer.

Getting loans and full-time jobs probably seem remote to you at this point. There's a sense in which that's true. It is highly unlikely that you'll need a business loan any time

In part, you're laying the foundation for future success by reaching out to people as a freshman.

soon. Nor will you likely apply for a full-time, professional level job for a while. You will still need help from people if you want to get the most out of college, which is to say that you need connections starting right now.

In part, you're laying the foundation for future success by reaching out to people as a freshman. As you near graduation you'll be asking professors for recommendations. Whom will you ask? If you haven't cultivated some good working relationships with teaching faculty, how will they be able to recommend you enthusiastically? Of course, you'll also want some professionals from your chosen field to say nice things about you. If you haven't connected with anyone during internships and co-op work, who will you have in your court?

Contacts don't have to be big shots or geezers. It's helpful to have good working relationships with other students too. You should know someone in every course you take who will share lecture notes if you have to miss class. Getting dates, rushing a fraternity, getting tickets to a ball game or concert—other students can help, but only if you know them. *This is particularly important if you're a commuter.* Moreover, other students can connect you with faculty and professionals who can help you solve a variety of problems. Additionally, every successful person was once a novice. The student sitting next to you in Freshman English might be the next Bill Gates or Madeleine Albright.

■ Mentors

When a more experienced person takes an ongoing, personal interest in your development, such a person is termed a mentor. Highly successful people often point to a key teacher or leader who advised, guided, supported, and pushed them on their way. Plato had Socrates. Aristotle had Plato. Bill Curry, who coached football at Georgia Tech, Alabama, and Kentucky, was coached over the course of his playing career by Bobby Dodd, Vince Lombardi, and Don Shula. If you're not a sports fan, that's analogous to learning music from Mozart, writing from Shakespeare, or chemistry from Madam Curie. Marian Wright Edelman's *Lanterns: A Memoir of Mentors* is an inspiring account of how both ordinary and famous people helped her grow from a poor black child in segregated South Carolina into an attorney with a Yale law degree and the founder of the Children's Defense Fund.

One of the best ways to learn something is by watching an expert do it right. Psychologists call this vicarious learning, and it's something you want to get as much of as is possible. Just think what it would be like for a budding engineer to apprentice to a Leonardo da Vinci, a novice manager to work for a Colin Powell, an aspiring politician to shadow a Governor Christie Whitman for an extended period. Obviously, not everyone can study at the feet of a master, but just about everyone can find teachers and leaders who are farther along the road to success than they are themselves. It could be a professor or dean. It could be an employer. It might be the senior down the hall who's the top pre-med on campus or who's already a successful student entrepreneur.

The trick is how to get these people to help out little old you? The first step is to forget the "little old you." So long as you see yourself as insignificant, you are undermining your attempts to build your success. You may not be as old or experienced as the person whose help you are seeking, but someone helped them along their way and today you'd like help on your way. And some day, it will be your turn to provide assistance to others as they build their success. Here are some suggestions for finding a mentor.

■ Steps in Forming a Mentor Relationship

1. *Show them you're committed to success.* Before people take you on as a protégé, they want to know that you're a winner. You've got to convince them you've got the talent and drive to make spending time with you worth their while.

   Representatives from student organizations often make requests of professors, civic leaders, and people in business. Will you teach our fraternity pledge class study skills? Can you give a talk on investment banking to our professional association? Could you conduct a resume workshop for our organization?

   Even if they're not particularly critical, we have observed that professionals automatically form impressions of every student who makes the request and handles the arrangements. Does the student ask far enough ahead of time for the expert to clear his schedule? If not, the professional will assume the student doesn't know how to manage his time. He will also resent the implication that he, the professional, has so little to do that, of course, he can adjust his schedule at the last minute for the convenience of the student.

   Has the student thought through her request carefully enough so that she can state it clearly? Notice the difference between: A.) Our group has a lot of liberal arts majors. Last year's seniors didn't do very well at finding good jobs. Could you talk to us about how we could improve our chances? and B.) We need someone to talk to us about getting good jobs. An expert will have a much better chance of delivering a timely, relevant message to group A than to Group B. She will also be inclined to regard the representative of group A as brighter, more conscientious, and more mature.

   Do the students follow through? Do they meet the speaker when she gets there? Do they have the overhead slide projector ready to go? Did they take the trouble to drum up a crowd? Do they send a letter of thanks? Is it well written? Since so many students fail to observe minimal standards of professional courtesy, you have to behave truly abysmally to distinguish yourself as a real loser. For the same reason, it is easy to show yourself to be a winner. By simply being considerate of the professionals you deal with, you stand out.

   Every college class you take provides you with an opportunity to demonstrate to a professor that you've got the "right stuff." Turning in quality work is an obvious first step, but don't stop there. Attend class and be punctual. Perhaps most important is that you participate in class. No, don't speak up just to hear yourself talk, but do contribute to the class discussion. If you don't understand something, ask for an explanation. An intelligent question usually gets a good answer. It also shows that you were intelligent for asking the question. Come prepared. If you've read yesterday's class notes and today's chapter, you're more prepared than most students. Your professors won't know this, however, unless you speak up.

   Many of you are attending large state universities and community colleges. Classes often have several hundred students in them. Graduating seniors sometimes can't identify a single professor who knows them well enough to write a decent recommendation. Don't get caught in that predicament. If you go to a big school, make it a point for at least one professor in your field to know you well and to think well of you.

You accomplish this by making an A and writing the best term paper or final exam the prof ever saw. At least that's what you try for. This should also be the class that you never miss and you're always prepared for. And no matter how shy you are, force yourself to participate in class discussions. You may not be someone with a 1300 SAT score and a 3.7 GPA. If you're working your way through school, you may not have much time for your studies. But surely you can concentrate doubly hard on at least one class.

Our university provides various ways for students to get to know professors. Every quarter hundreds of students "Take a Prof to Lunch" for just $5. Others participate in a "Faculty Friends" program. On the other hand, there are thousands who do neither. Nor do they stay after class to pursue a topic, show up at the various lecture series, or drop by a professor's office for advice.

When I (Bill) was in professional school, there was an especially engaging and eminent professor from whom I wanted to learn more. Some of my fellow students shared my interest in having more contact with this person. We asked him if he would have lunch with us so we could talk. He graciously consented. This grew into a tradition. Several times a year we would gather in my tiny efficiency apartment and pepper Dr. Harvey with questions. It was one of the most stimulating educational experiences I've ever had in my life. Some years later it was Dr. Harvey whom I asked to recommend me for my PhD program. In his letter of recommendation he introduced me to the admissions committee by noting that I had started the lunch and learn group.

The same principles apply on the job. Remember Chapter 7. Whether you're co-oping, interning, or working part-time—show someone in power that you're serious about building success. No, not by apple-polishing, brown-nosing, or toadying. As the saying goes, "You do it the old-fashioned way. You earn it." You earn it by showing up on time every day, working hard, and volunteering for extra work.

2. *Make it worth their while.* When you search for a mentor, you're looking for someone who will teach you, guide you, and help you. It's nice if someone volunteers for the job, but most people you'd want to learn from are busy, busy, busy. Usually they'll help you if you help them. Generally it's up to you to take the first step.

Volunteer to assist your prospective mentor with his work. Many professors do research and could use someone to tally scores or collate data. Out on the job, managers, project engineers, head nurses, etc. can generally use a helping hand. So can presidents of sororities, professional societies, and student governments. When you do volunteer to help, do your best. Do a bang-up job. Go the second mile. Demonstrate some loyalty.

3. *Expect the relationship to evolve gradually.* It usually takes a while for a mentor to warm up to you enough to take you under her wing. And after a solid relationship is established, it should continue to evolve. As you learn more and more from your mentor, you should gradually be accorded greater responsibility. The idea is to work toward becoming a colleague, not a lackey.

It sometimes happens that your prospective mentor doesn't want to take you on. No matter how hard you try, (s)he brushes you off . Try not to take it personally. Maybe (s)he's too busy, (s)he's already mentoring too many other aspiring students, or (s)he's just not a very helpful person.

At some point, your persistence becomes bullheadedness, and you're better off trying with someone else. Not everyone can have Bill Gates or Elizabeth Dole for a mentor. Nor is the biggest big shot around necessarily your best prospect. Generally, a less prominent person has more time to give and a better disposition for doing so.

As you become more successful yourself, don't forget all the help you got along the way. One of the best ways to show your gratitude is by helping those who are just starting their own journey.

■ Summary

1. It's to your advantage to have a network of contacts.
2. It's up to you to build the network.
3. Start your freshman year.
4. Establish relationships with successful people by showing them you're committed to success and by helping them.
5. Cultivate relationships with professors, professionals in your field, and other students.
6. You can find helpful people in many places, including: classes, professional organizations, campus activities, and at work.
7. Develop a filing system for keeping track of your contacts.
8. If possible, cultivate a relationship with a mentor who will help guide you on your road to success.

■ Networking Exercise

An oft repeated bit of wisdom is that you're within seven phone calls of contacting anyone in the world. Suppose you wanted to reach Tony Blair, Prime Minister of Great Britain. You'd contact the most important politician you knew—maybe your hometown mayor. She'd put you in touch with a state senator who would put you in touch with someone in the governor's office who would put you in touch with the governor who would put you in touch with a U.S. senator knowledgeable about foreign affairs who would get you to a State Department official who would get you to the prime minister.

That's kind of how you look for jobs, contacts, and favorable recommendations. You go out looking to see who knows who.

Fill out the list below, checking those positions for which you know a particular person currently employed.

Mark your answers **in pencil**

_____ Investment Counselor	_____ Diplomat/State Department
_____ Landscape Architect	_____ Physical Therapist
_____ Accountant	_____ Chemist
_____ Real Estate Sales	_____ Journalist
_____ Contractor	_____ Alum working for a major corp.
_____ Computer Scientist	_____ Mathematician/Statistician
_____ Urban Planner	_____ Physician
_____ Retail Manager	_____ Banker
_____ Engineer	_____ Public Relations Worker
_____ Personnel Director	_____ User-friendly tutor
_____ Law Officer	_____ Geologist
_____ Lawyer	_____ Military Officer
_____ Architect	_____ Systems Analyst
_____ Industrial Designer	_____ Adult Educator/Corporate Training
_____ Physicist	_____ Advertiser
_____ Marketing Researcher	_____ Pilot
_____ Alum who's an Entrepreneur	_____ Writer
_____ Technical Sales	_____ Environmental Engineer/Scientist
_____ Psychologist/Counselor	_____ Business Consultant
_____ Small Business Owner	_____ _____
_____ _____	_____ _____

Now in small groups, take out a pen and compare lists. Check off in **ink** the additional professional contacts possible if you use the resources available to you through your association with group members. Note how your network grows.

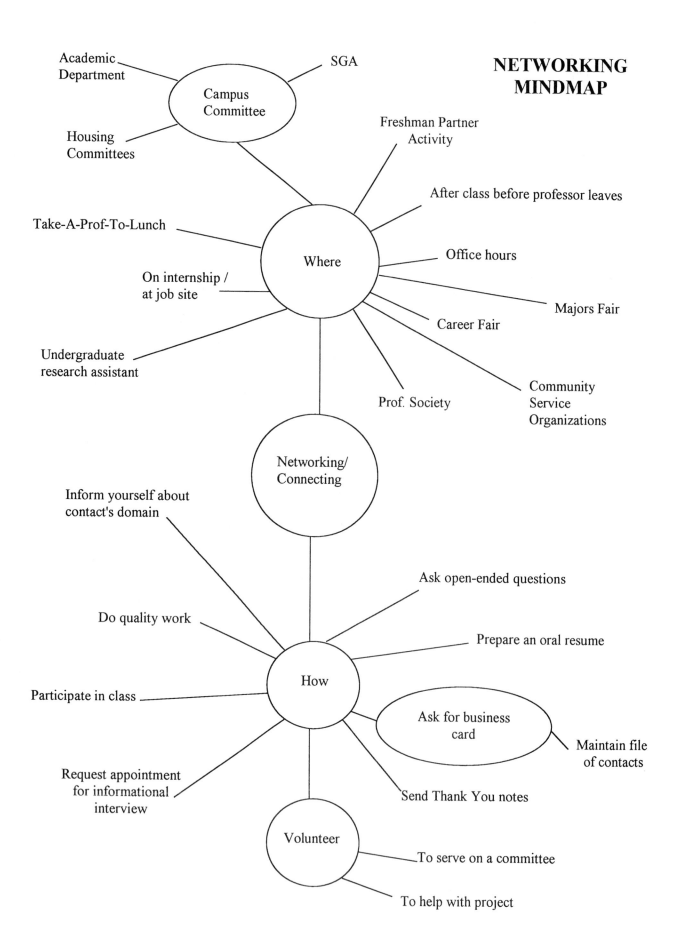

NETWORKING MINDMAP

Academic Department

SGA

Campus Committee

Housing Committees

Freshman Partner Activity

After class before professor leaves

Take-A-Prof-To-Lunch

Where

Office hours

On internship / at job site

Majors Fair

Career Fair

Undergraduate research assistant

Prof. Society

Community Service Organizations

Networking/ Connecting

Inform yourself about contact's domain

Ask open-ended questions

Do quality work

Prepare an oral resume

How

Participate in class

Ask for business card

Maintain file of contacts

Request appointment for informational interview

Send Thank You notes

Volunteer

To serve on a committee

To help with project

CHAPTER 8
The Anatomy of Achievement

How do high achievers do it? What makes them tick? Is it possible for me to become a high achiever?

There is no magic to achievement. High achievers operate in characteristic ways and think in consistent patterns that lead to their success. You can learn to think and act like a high achiever. If you do, you'll get similar results.

Psychologist David McClelland has probably studied the achievement motive more thoroughly than any other scholar. In *The Achievement Motive* and *The Achieving Society*, he describes the mindset and the behavioral patterns of the typical high achiever.

Goal Focus. First, achievers are focused on goals. Nor will just any goal do. The goal must be related to achievement—winning in a competition, creating a better widgit, starting a successful business, attaining excellence. Finding new friends is a worthwhile goal, but it has to do with affiliative needs, not the need to achieve. Attaining inner peace is arguably as an important a goal as there is. It is not, however, an achievement goal; it's a spiritual goal. Achievers think about their goals a great deal of the time. They often fantasize about reaching them. They may also worry about not reaching them. They picture their sense of satisfaction upon bringing their goals to fruition. They also think about the sense of disappointment they would suffer if they failed.

Goals That Challenge. Achievers set realistic, but not easy goals. Their goals demand talent and effort, but they are do-able. The most successful people don't generally take long shots. They don't depend on luck. Because they believe they will work harder and smarter than their competitors, they like a difficult challenge. They are not gamblers, however, because they don't like to compete in any arena in which the outcome is primarily determined by chance.

One way psychologists have studied achievement is to watch subjects compete at a ring-toss game. The game works as follows. Participants are given the opportunity to practice briefly tossing rings over a peg. The greater distance from the peg that the participant stands, the more points are awarded for a successful toss. Of course, the greater the distance from the peg, the more difficult it is to ring the peg. Participants can stand next to the peg and score every time; they just won't be awarded many points. Or participants can stand at the other end of the room. If they score, they are awarded major points, but their chances of scoring are remote. Players who throw from medium range almost always win the most points. And here is the interesting part. They also reveal the highest drive for success on other measures. And, most importantly, they tend to be the best students, the most effective salespeople, the most successful entrepreneurs.

What this research suggests is that underachievers go after ridiculously easy goals or impossibly difficult ones. Achievers like a challenge, but they don't want to be overwhelmed. They aim for goals of moderate difficulty. Then, as soon as they reach them, they set their sights one notch higher.

Achievers set clear goals. There is a difference between dreams and plans. Anyone can fantasize about fame and fortune, but a plan requires concrete, specific objectives to shoot for. The most effective people take the trouble to make their goals clear. Too many students say, "I'm going to get a lot of studying done this weekend," or "I want to make it big in the business world."

The true achievers more likely say, "I'm going to study history for two hours Saturday morning and work math problems for two hours on Sunday afternoon," or "I'm going to major in electrical engineering so I can eventually develop computer hardware." When you set clear goals, you can tell whether you're really making progress. If you are, success is a powerful motivator. If not, you can adjust your plans.

Achievers Strive. Achievers take action. They are not content merely to contemplate their goals; they work actively to reach them. They work hard, and they work smart. They strategize and plan. Then they follow their strategy and implement their plan. They are very conscious of their time and guard it jealously. Efficiency is important to them. They spend time and energy building skills which will enhance their chances for goal attainment.

Achievement oriented athletes practice diligently to build up their basic sports skills. While Michael Jordan was a remarkable athlete, he has been described as highly competitive and exceedingly disciplined. Without his extra hours of practice, he would not have been able to accomplish all that he did on the basketball court. Similarly, successful scientists build strong mathematical and research skills, then spend long hours in the laboratory in order to make their scientific discoveries. The most successful business people are typically very hard workers who constantly are refining their skills—learning new computer applications, acquiring new management techniques, studying their competition, building up their core competencies.

So, how can you become a high achieving student? Master basic learning skills. Learn to read faster and with better comprehension. Build a strong vocabulary. Improve your ability to write clearly and concisely. Know how to use the library. Master mathematics. Learn new computer applications as they become available. And study, study, study. It's really quite simple to become a good student. You do so through hard work. (I said it was simple. I didn't say it was easy.)

Receptive to Help. David McClelland's research revealed that high achievers frequently made use of expert help. In fact, expecting to be helped was a standard feature of the high achiever's mental outlook. This may seem like a paradox, but it isn't. Achievers ARE self-reliant and independent. They accept the fact they are responsible for their own success. They do not, however, regard themselves as omnipotent or invulnerable. Therefore, they are willing to ask for help. They don't regard getting help as a sign of weakness or anything to be apologetic about. One of the ways achievers get help is by cultivating relationships with people who have useful resources or expertise. When it comes to reaching their goals, achievers would rather spend time with an unfriendly expert than with an inexpert friend. This doesn't mean that achievers don't have inexpert friends. It just means they don't rely on a friend for technical advice if the friend has no technical expertise.

Because achievers want to succeed, they tend to associate with successful people. You might find it revealing to reflect on your circle of friends. Are they ambitious? Serious about succeeding? Hardworking? Conscientious students? If none of them is, then you will probably find it harder to operate like an achiever, yourself. I don't mean to suggest that there is no room for unconventional or quirky people in your life, but who will help you if you surround yourself with people who aren't strongly motivated to achieve. Who will be a serious member of your study group? Who will support you for being a hard worker who aspires to academic success?

One of the surest ways to learn the ropes is from people who have mastered their craft. Apprenticing yourself to someone who has already succeeded is an excellent strategy. Suppose you wanted to become a physician. Then find a junior or senior with a high GPA who has worked summers in a hospital and knows what it takes to get into medical school. See Chapter 7 for tips on finding a mentor.

The other way in which high achievers get help is by asking for it from the appropriate office or department. Most students are surprised when they learn about all the services that are available to them. We recommend that, at your earliest convenience, you carefully review your student handbook or the appropriate section of your college catalog. Then start using your campus resources. If your school doesn't offer a service that you need, see if you can find it elsewhere. Remember, it's up to you to get whatever assistance you require to succeed. Nobody is going to rescue you. Achievers are acutely aware of this fact, so they actively seek out whatever help they need in order to succeed.

Achievers Overcome Barriers. When they run into roadblocks, they keep trying till they find a way to get around them. Naturally, they can get discouraged too, but they bounce back from defeat rather than letting it keep them down. Not all obstacles are external. If personal shortcomings hold achievers back, they find a way to compensate, or they change. They never wait to be rescued. They actively seek out expert help whenever it's needed to get the job done.

One of our greatest satisfactions is watching college students develop. We've seen country bumpkins overcome their lack of sophistication. We've seen shy students join clubs so they can learn to conduct a meeting. We've known pre-meds who managed to eke out B's in calculus because they studied overtime and hired a tutor.

Successful people come in all shapes and sizes. One thing they have in common is that they don't easily take "no" for an answer. They're not quick to throw in the towel. They encounter their share of setbacks, but they keep on keeping on.

We recall one young woman from a rural background whose father had died when she was a child. Her mother discouraged her from applying to a competitive college. She filled out the forms by herself and also applied for financial aid. Happily, she was accepted. When she arrived on campus, she felt out of place, and she had to struggle to survive in class. Her boyfriend kept after her to transfer to the junior college in her hometown. Besides, who needed a college degree? She could always clerk in the local dime store. With some difficulty, she broke things off with her old boyfriend. She joined a study group, and that helped her with her grades. She got counseling to improve her self-confidence. She had to work part-time to make ends meet. At first, she waited tables, but eventually she did drafting for a small engineering company. She finally managed to graduate and began working full-time for the same firm.

It wasn't a very good job. Her attempts at finding a better one didn't lead to much, so she got help from her college's career planning center. She developed a better job search plan and improved her resume. She was discouraged to discover she was no longer eligible to set up interviews through the campus placement center. But she didn't give up. She began dropping by the placement office at noon and started having lunch with the corporate recruiters. Within a few months she had been invited to interview with several companies. She received several offers and accepted the one she felt was best for her.

We are proud to know this woman who was born into near poverty. Her family and friends advised her against pursuing her dreams. She made mistakes, and she encountered innumerable barriers to success. But she didn't give up.

Today, she is an engineer for a Fortune 500 corporation, involved in the design of supersonic aircraft.

■ The Consequences of Achievement Motivation

In *The Achieving Society*, McLelland discusses the impact of the achiever's mindset upon society over the ages and across cultures. He analyzed the literature and folk tales of ancient Greece over a period of some hundreds of years. Whenever the themes cited above appeared consistently in the literature, Greece flourished economically. When those themes were absent in Grecian culture, the Greek economy suffered. These findings were replicated when McLelland investigated other civilizations, both ancient and modern.

Those cultures, then, which successfully promote the achiever's mindset will tend to be productive societies with expanding economies. For individuals who embrace the achiever's mindset, they will tend to be productive and successful, at least within certain fields. Students who think like achievers make better grades. Achievement oriented entrepreneurs are more likely to succeed in their business ventures. Salespeople with the achiever's mindset generate more sales than those who don't embrace that mindset.

The relationship between your mindset and your success is not perfectly predictable. Moreover, your mindset is not the only factor that influences results. Luck and inborn talent are also factors, but *all things being equal* the achievement oriented person will be more successful. The same is true for a society.

You cannot influence your luck, nor can you change the talent pool with which you were endowed. You can, however, cultivate an achiever's mindset. You can focus on goals and reaching them in spite of whatever obstacles arise. If you do, you'll more likely succeed. McClelland's research found that people could, in fact, learn to think like achievers. When they did, they became more successful. As one successful person put it, "The harder and smarter I worked, the luckier I got!"

■ How To Get More Go

What if you're not maximizing your potential? What if you're not achieving very much of what you want to achieve? Suppose you've taken an honest look in the mirror and see someone who is more passive than active, someone who will not go far unless you make some changes. If you've taken the College Adjustment Inventory and your Achievement score is low, this could be you Well, don't despair. You can change.

Research psychologist George Burris taught underachieving college students some of the same principles that are outlined in this chapter. In just one semester he got results. Achievement motivation scores went up, and so did grades. How did he accomplish this? He taught them to think like achievers. One of his techniques was to teach his subjects to write stories rich in achievement themes. You can try it on for size yourself. Get a pencil and paper and write a very short story which starts with the following sentence stem: "Pat was studying for finals when . . . " Give yourself five minutes to complete the story. You can refer to the following diagram to help you score your story for achievement imagery.

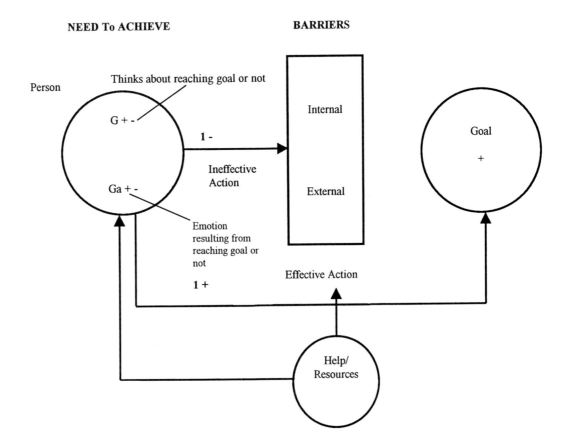

1. First, there has to be a desire for reaching an achievement-related goal. Did Pat want to make an A? Hope to be first in his/her class? Want the A so as to gain access to a competitive graduate program? Want to master core material that was needed for professional success? All these are examples of a need for achievement. IF a story has this element, you give yourself a point AND are eligible to score additional points if you have any of the other elements depicted in the graphic above.

2. Does Pat think about reaching the goal or not?

3. Does Pat experience emotion at the prospect of reaching the goal (e.g., satisfaction) or not (e.g., frustration)?

4. Are there references to using ineffective methods to reach the goal? Examples would include weak effort, outdated techniques, cutting corners, etc.

5. Are there references to using effective methods to reach the goal? Examples would include putting in extra effort, employing proven skills and techniques.

6. Are there references to internal or external barriers to goal achievement?

7. Is there a reference to a helpful person who will assist Pat to reach the goal?

■ Example of Achievement-Rich Story

So what can you do if you want to achieve more? First, as simple as it sounds, you've got to believe that your own efforts make a difference.

Chris was frustrated. He very much wanted to get an internship with NASA, but all the interview slots were already filled for this semester. Moreover, Chris was rather shy and not very confident that he could give an interview that would convince the NASA representative to hire him. He was tempted to forget about his aspiration to work for NASA, but he decided he was going to do everything possible to make his dream come true.

The next day he went to Career Services and got an appointment with one of the counselors. He explained his predicament, and the counselor suggested that he wait in the reception area just before noon and ask to join the NASA representative for lunch to talk about employment opportunities. The counselor also helped Chris develop a good resume and even conducted a mock interview with him. By the time Chris was finished working with the counselor, he felt much more confident about himself and more optimistic about his prospects.

On the day the NASA woman was in town Chris got up earlier than usual and practiced answering the questions his counselor had posed. He attended his morning classes and then headed for the Career Services office. He had on a clean shirt and tie and his resume in hand. Although he was a bit nervous, he approached the recruiter when she appeared and she graciously accepted his offer to take her to lunch. She told him she was impressed with his forwardness in asking to meet her. She looked forward to discussing internship opportunities with him over lunch.

In this brief vignette, it is clear that Chris has a goal—NASA. He's frustrated (Ga+) because of the difficulties (barriers, both internal and external) he's having in reaching his goal. He's tempted to give in to his shyness and settle for something else, but then he determines to overcome his shyness and surmount the difficulty of no available interview slots (I+). He gets help from a counselor (Help/resources) and practices what she showed him (I+). He connects with the NASA rep, and things look promising for an internship.

High achievers think about reaching goals in spite of obstacles much of the time. Getting help, improving performance, and overcoming obstacles are enduring features of their mental landscape. If you learn to think similarly you, too will become a high achiever.

■ Locus of Control

Locus of control is a concept developed by the psychologist, Julian Rotter. Rotter observed that individuals tend to attribute the course of their lives to either internal or external causes. Did I make an A on the test because I studied hard or because the test was easy? Will I get a good job because I've developed marketable skills, cultivated good contacts, and practiced interviewing or because some long lost relative will somehow remember me and decide to offer me a great position with his multinational corporation. Do I advance in life because of effort and skill or because of luck, fate, and circumstance? Locus of control is considered to be on a continuum. One tends toward the internal or the external. The consequences of one's tendency are profound.

African American college students with an internal locus of control were more likely to participate in the social protests which led to civil rights legislation than were more externally oriented peers. School children with an internal locus of control were more likely to defer gratification for a larger reward whereas externally oriented children were content to accept a much smaller reward given immediately. Tuberculosis patients with an internal locus of control turned out to know a lot more about the causes and cures of their disease than did more externally oriented patients. Internally oriented college students retained more material which they had read from a public policy document than externally oriented college students. Think about the implications of these various findings: Internals are better citizens and are more likely to improve society. Internals can defer gratification in order to earn a larger reward. Internals better understand their difficulties and will thus be better able to address them. Internals are better informed. Thus they can operate their lives based upon better information. Some theorists have argued that much of what we call intelligence and effective coping behavior is inextricably tied up with having an internal locus of control.

Another psychologist, Richard DeCharms, worked with teachers of disadvantaged children. He emphasized that they work to develop an internal locus of control in their students, and the students' grades improved significantly. DeCharms has developed an innovative way of thinking about locus of control and achievement. He says people tend to be either Pawns or Origins. Pawns are passive, generally acted upon, and don't have much control over their future. Origins, on the other hand, actively determine what happens to them.

You can take the Pawn analogy one step further—individuals can be compared to the pieces in the game of chess. A pawn is the least powerful piece. Basically, a pawn can move straight ahead, one square at a time. It enjoys very little choice or power. When confronted with an obstacle, it can only wait until the obstacle is removed. If however, a pawn is passed all the way to the end of the board, it can be exchanged for a queen. A queen can move vertically, horizontally, or diagonally. It can go forward or backward for as many squares as there are on the board. Talk about controlling your own destiny! The queen has the whole board to play with. The pawn has just one square.

Suppose a queen mistakenly thought she was a pawn. Her choices would be drastically limited. Conversely, if a pawn started acting like a queen, the sky would be the limit. Why do some people become pawns and others become queens? Why do some students feel powerless to influence their futures, while others are convinced their efforts can make a difference?

Any kind of oppression undermines the development of motivation. Oppression can be blatant, like racism or poverty. It can be as subtle as overprotective parents. But it's too late to change where you grew up or how your parents raised you. So what can you do if you want to achieve more? There is a ten-word phrase which contains the secret of your success. Just to make it more challenging, each of the ten words is a two-letter word. The fifth and tenth words rhyme. Can you create the phrase? The phrase appears at the end of this chapter.

We believe the foundation of all achievement lies in the firm belief that planning and effort can influence the future. So, are you the kind of person who lays plans to open a business in five years? Or do you figure, "Why bother? Something will go wrong. It always does." Can you pass up the Monday Night Movie in order to fine tune your resume? Or do you think, "It's not worth it. You've got to have connections to work for that company." Do you study harder after a bad grade? Or do you say, "It doesn't do any good to prepare for that teacher's tests anyway."

So what can you do if you want to achieve more? First, as simple as it sounds, you've got to believe that your own efforts make a difference. If we haven't convinced you, please talk to a counselor. Virtually all counselors are committed to helping their clients become more independent, more in charge of their own lives.

Second, follow the suggestions in this book. We didn't pull them out of a hat. Our ideas come directly from the experts on achievement motivation. Most chapters have to do with planning, setting goals, organizing, developing skills, and using resources. We can't make you follow our suggestions, but we urge you to try them. They work. Your performance will improve. You'll taste success. And success breeds success. We guarantee it.

If you'd like another way to examine your own motive to achieve, see the "Quick Scoring Achievement Motivation Survey" at the end of this chapter.

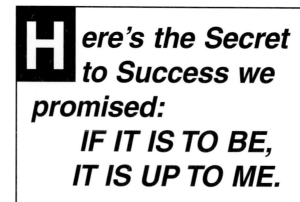

Here's the Secret to Success we promised:
IF IT IS TO BE,
IT IS UP TO ME.

Name: _____ Date: _____

■ Quick-Scoring Achievement Motivation Quiz

Points   *Score*

1. <u>0</u>   I have no clear goals in life.
    <u>1</u>   I have a general idea of a career in which I want to succeed.
    <u>2</u>   I set daily objectives which advance me toward my long-term goals.
    <u>3</u>   I set daily, weekly, and quarterly goals which will advance me toward my
             long-term goals.   _____

2. <u>0</u>   I'm too proud to accept help, no matter how stuck or lost I get.
    <u>1</u>   I will accept help, but only when it's offered.
    <u>2</u>   I actively seek out expert help whenever I get stuck or lost.
    <u>3</u>   I am acquainted with most campus resources and regularly use them
             without becoming dependent upon them.   _____

3. <u>0</u>   I tend to give up after the first setback.
    <u>1</u>   I eventually bounce back from a setback after a period of immobilization.
    <u>2</u>   I analyze my setbacks instead of kicking myself or blaming others.
    <u>3</u>   A setback inspires me to try again, using new methods if needed.   _____

4. <u>0</u>   My fantasies about career success are limited to scenes from "Lifestyles of
             the Rich and Famous."
    <u>1</u>   My fantasies about career success include practical details of my future
             world of work.
    <u>2</u>   My fantasies about career success include thinking about steps I can take
             on a daily basis.
    <u>3</u>   My fantasies about career success include long-range, intermediate, and
             daily plans to reach my goals.   _____

5. <u>0</u>   Most of my goals are so high that I seldom reach them or so low that
             I reach them with very little effort.
    <u>1</u>   At least some of my goals are moderately difficult—high enough to
             challenge me but low enough not to overwhelm me with anxiety.
    <u>2</u>   Most of my goals are moderately difficult.
    <u>3</u>   Most of my goals are moderately difficult, and I increase their difficulty as
             I reach them.   _____

    TOTAL   _____

Scoring:

    0   Points   If you don't crawl out from under the doormat and start moving, your future appears dim.
 1–5   Points   You're taking the first steps toward success. Still a ways to go though.
6–10   Points   You're on the way, but watch out—success can be addictive.
11–15 Points   The stuff of champions. You're on your way to succeeding big time.

CHAPTER 9
The Resilient Student

"Just when you get both ends to meet, somebody moves one of the ends." This was one of my father's favorite expressions. With each passing year, I realize more fully how vividly it captures the fact that life is a struggle. This doesn't mean that life has to be miserable. It DOES imply that you will be miserable if you don't accept that a certain amount of struggle is each human's destiny. You must confront challenges, overcome barriers, and rebound from setbacks every day of your life. At any rate, you must do so if you plan to build success. Building success is hard work. It is worthwhile, but it is, nonetheless, a challenge.

Not every professor is inspiring, nor does every class come easy, nor does every project fall readily into place. Roommates aren't perfect, nor are classmates. Sometimes the book you need is already checked out, the loan you needed doesn't come through, and the tests all fall on the same day. Eventually, you'll find that bosses, colleagues, customers, and subordinates also lack perfection and can be sources of frustration.

Reflect for a minute on the issues you'll be facing in the 21st Century: ongoing, rapid change, information overload, dealing with people unlike yourself, complicated career paths, and enormous societal problems. Every one of these phenomena can be stressful, but change—rapid, constant change—is, we believe, the reality underlying all of these issues. You'll be expected to produce more in less time. You must constantly be learning new skills. You must acquire the facility of working comfortably with an incredibly diverse work force. Whatever job security you possess will come from your own resourcefulness and expertise. The 21st Century is not for the faint of heart!

Since you don't have any other century available to you, you'd best gear up. Here is what we know about resilience and coping with change.

■ Psychological Hardiness

In the 1970's, Salvatore Maddi and Suzanne Kobasa studied executives undergoing stress. More specifically, they studied a group of managers and executives in a large corporation which was undergoing reorganization. Reorganization means many jobs will change, and more than a few will be lost. In companies that reorganize, morale goes down and anxiety goes up. Will I have to change jobs? Will I have to let good people go? Will I be out on the street myself? If you keep up with the news at all, you know that corporate downsizing remains a landmine for employees in the American workplace. (It turns out that the work of Maddi and Kobasa is extremely relevant to the students of today and the workers of tomorrow.)

During reorganization and downsizing, more people tend to get sick. They get more colds and cases of influenza. They get more migraines and backaches. And they have more ulcers and heart attacks. That's the bad news. The good news is that not everybody is equally vulnerable. Maddi and Kobasa found that some individuals were "psychologically hardy" (PH). These hardy individuals were sick less often and bounced back sooner after their illness. What makes them tick? The researchers identified several basic attitudes common to hardy individuals. You can think of them as the three C's:

1. An openness to **change**, viewing change as a challenge rather than a threat.
2. A high degree of **commitment** to what they do, demonstrating involvement in their activities and evidently relating them to life goals and objectives. Subjects low in commitment tended to be alienated from work, people, and social institutions.
3. A sense of **control** over most events encountered in life, rather than helplessness. High PH subjects were convinced they could influence the course of their lives. They believed their efforts made a difference at work, in school, and with other people. Low PH individuals were convinced they were powerless to influence outcomes. They tended to attribute what happened in their lives to forces outside themselves.

As you can see from the diagram below, individuals can respond to stressful events by coping actively or passively. High PH people see change as a challenge, make a commitment to get involved, and believe they have power to manage a difficult situation. Conversely, low PH people see change as a threat, avoid involvement, and feel powerless to cope. This leads them to deny the problems they face. They generally avoid their difficulties rather than confront them.

Hi PH	Stressors	Lo PH
Active Coping		Passive Coping
See Challenge	Change	See Threat
Commitment	Daily Activities	Alienation
Empowered	Control of One's Life	Powerlessness

Change, obstacles, setbacks, and adversity are an inextricable part of living. The psychologically hardy person knows this, expects it, and thrives on actively engaging life. Every day brings new situations to handle, tasks to complete, events to manage. The high PH person meets life actively:

Meets problems head on, doesn't escape, evade, or avoid.
Believes struggle pays off, wrking hard and smart pays.
Believes (s)he has power to influence the outcome.
Focuses on the situation.

The less psychologically hardy person meets life more passively:

Runs from problems, escapes, evades, avoids, denies, blames.
Is quick to give up. Doubts working harder or smarter pays.
Doubts (s)he has the power to influence the outcome.
Worries about the outcome.

In general, it is helpful to believe that you can manage the situation, solve the problem, climb the mountain. In one experiment, group A were asked to come up with as many solutions to a problem as they could. The one with the most viable solutions would be paid $10. Group B were asked to come up with X number of solutions (where X = average number of solutions of group A + 5). Group B reached significantly more viable solutions than Group A. Because the instructions implied they COULD reach more good solutions, they did. Some say defining a problem as a "problem" makes it harder to solve. Define it instead as a situation.

■ Learned Helplessness and Learned Optimism

Learned Helplessness (LH) is a term coined by psychologist Martin Seligman. LH is a condition that develops after situations in which one's behavior has no impact on the outcome of the goal toward which the behavior is directed. There is a lot of research on this topic, some of it with human subjects, some with animals.

You might wonder what possible relevance animal research has for you. The answer is that much (though not all) human behavior is very similar to the behavior of "lower" animals. We have some good ideas about the ways in which human emotional problems develop from analyzing Pavlov's famous classical conditioning experiments with dogs. Frequently, researchers start with lower animals, replicate their studies with primates, and finally study humans. As you read the brief research summaries below, try to see the analogies between the situations of the animals and human situations. Here are just a few of the relevant studies:

1. Dogs were placed in one of two treatments:
   A. Harnessed and subject to electric shock. No matter how hard they struggled, they could not escape.
   B. Harnessed and subject to electric shock. If they struggled, they could escape.
   Dogs in the A treatment developed LH. They became less aggressive, less competitive, and less able to escape other aversive situations. Dogs in the B treatment became more competitive, more aggressive when the situation required it, and better able to escape from other aversive situations.

2. Similar experiments were run with field mice. An experimenter would hold a mouse in his hand. In one condition the animal was not permitted to escape until it stopped struggling. In the other condition, the mouse was repeatedly allowed to escape, then recaptured, then allowed to escape again. After receiving one or the other of these two treatments each mouse was placed in a tub of water. The mice whose struggles led to escape swam approximately 50 times longer than those who had been prevented from escaping. The mice who were able to exercise some control over their experimental situation generalized their "empowerment" and coped better with other challenges.

3. Human subjects were placed in a situation simulating a math class. All subjects were asked to solve mathematical problems. The subjects in one condition were consistently told that their solutions were wrong. The subjects in the other condition were told that most of their solutions were correct. On future tests, the second group of subjects consistently performed better on problem solving tasks than did the subjects in the first condition.

   It is important to bear in mind that it is not just having bad things happen to you from which you cannot escape that causes learned helplessness. The key is for there to be a break in the connection between behavior and outcome.

4. For example, in a different kind of experiment, one group of rats were fed only when they pressed a bar. Another group of rats were fed randomly, independently of any bar pressing. The first group of rats became more active and better learners. The other group, by comparison, were less active and learned less well.

5. A similar experiment replicated the outcome with pigeons.

Once an animal has LH, it is difficult to empower it. One technique is to force the animal through the steps required to effect the desired change. For example, a dog could be forced repeatedly out of its harness so that it would escape a shock. After many trials it starts to struggle on its own.

LH seems to impair animals and people in three ways:

1. Reduces motivation, energy, the will to struggle, solve problems, and survive.
2. Makes learning more difficult. Subjects ignore or seem unable to profit from information that would help it to escape or solve an important problem.
3. Increases emotional/physical distress. LH subjects are more anxious and depressed, more likely to have ulcers.

LH, then, is the acquired condition in which a subject behaves as though his or her responses have no impact on the outcome.

In Seligman's more recent work, *Learned Optimism*, he has refined his theory. He is persuaded that the cognitive mechanism through which LH is maintained in humans is a pessimistic frame of mind. Pessimism develops because of experiences in our daily lives that are analogous to those endured by the animals and humans in the various LH experiments cited above. Pessimism also flourishes when parents and other societal authority figures are pessimistic. Once individuals develop a pessimistic frame of mind, they tend to explain what happens to them quite differently than optimistic persons. Psychologists call this an attributional style, how you interpret what happens to you. It is comprised of three distinct dimensions.

1. **Personalization.** Are the causes of your life's events external or internal? For pessimists, "bad" things happen because of personal weakness or error. "It's my fault. I was lazy, stupid, inattentive, etc." If something good happens, it was luck, chance, or because of somebody else's efforts. For optimists, the reverse is true. They take credit for the good and explain the bad as not under their control.

2. **Permanence.** Are the significant events in your life temporary or permanent? "Always" and "never" suggest permanence. "Sometimes" and "lately" imply temporality. For a pessimist, misfortune is regarded as likly to endure. If something good happens, it is believed to be temporary. For optimists, the opposite is the case. Bad things are the result of a quirk or an off day. Good events will last or be repeated.

3. **Pervasiveness.** This dimension refers to the scope or generality of an event. For pessimists, negative events are regarded as pervasive. If something good happens, it is regarded as very limited in scope. For optimists, the reverse is true. A pessimist would suspect ALL professors to be unfair after unfair treatment from one. An optimist would figure it was only this particular prof who was a jerk.

In summary, optimists and pessimists interpret the events in their lives differently. Pessimists think that negative events are their own fault, will last forever, and will strike many aspects of their lives. Conversely, they think that good fortune was not of their own doing, will soon be gone, and is confined to this one instance.

Optimists, on the other hand, take credit for their successes, expect them to recur, and believe they will spread to other areas of their lives. Conversely, they disown their failures, figure their failures will soon pass, and assume they will be isolated to this one instance.

It turns out that individuals who have learned to be optimistic in their attributions tend to get very different results out of life. They tend to be more successful in school, in sports, at work, and in health. This is apparently because optimistic people tend to be more resilient, persistent, and undaunted in the face of setbacks. They are also more confident in their own abilities and see more opportunities throughout their world and over time.

In other words, **your** attributional style influences **your** likelihood of success now while you're in school and later in life as a professional, a citizen, and a member of a family. Working through the exercises at the end of this chapter will help you to understand hardiness and helplessness better.

■ Maintaining Perspective

We assume that you want to build your own success. You want a bright future, and this book tells you how to do it. Just remember, success is different for each person. Money and prestige don't guarantee success in the broadest sense of the word. Don't make the mistake of majoring in Pre-Wealth! At least not to the exclusion of everything else.

Occasionally, students ask us which branch of engineering offers the highest salaries. A few of these students want to choose their life's work on the basis of dollars alone. Actually, this doesn't even make good financial sense. The demand for graduates in different fields changes from year to year. Right now computer science is hot. It may not be ten years from now. How ironic it would be to commit to a field you hate and have it dry up on you before you turn thirty.

Besides, extrinsic rewards less often foster creative results than intrinsic ones. Research by Brandeis University's Teresa Amabile indicates that being interested in your work may be the single most important factor in a creative outcome. And it is the creative results that bring in top dollar. So learn to live with the following paradox: working only for money often stifles creativity; yet creativity is usually rewarded monetarily. We think it's smart to consider the financial prospects a field offers, but not to the exclusion of everything else. Find work that you like. It will pay off in many ways.

Focusing solely on the steps of your career ladder tends to produce tunnel vision. In today's rapidly changing world you need a broader view in order to be successful in your profession and in life. You need the liberal arts, social sciences, and fine arts as well as business and technical knowledge. You need more than smarts—you need wisdom.

If it is unwise to equate success with income, it is equally unwise to make your self-worth equal to your success. To do so breeds fear of failure, and that undermines your willingness to take risks. If you cannot respect yourself after a failure, you can expect anxiety, depression, and stress as your constant companions. Some students panic when they first see the Four-Year Master Plan. How can they possibly get everything done? They feel overwhelmed.

Remember, there is no "must" in the Master Plan. You don't HAVE to do any of it. If you manage to pull off half of it, you are probably well ahead of most other college students. The Master Plan is not an end in itself; it is only a set of guidelines. And when all is said and done they boil down to a few practical suggestions: Get organized. Whether you study five hours a week or twenty-five, use the most effective techniques. Clarify your goals. Get some work experience. Make some contacts. Use your campus resources. Learn how to find a job.

You can be competitive without becoming hooked on competition for its own sake. Some of you may prefer being a bigger fish in a smaller pond. Is an Ivy League degree really worth it if you have to wreck your family's finances to get it? Not everyone is necessarily happier at Microsoft than at Joe's Electronics. There are successful graduates who go into law, medicine, and engineering. Others join the Peace Corps, teach public school or enter social work. Still others practice their craft in an artist's studio or on a stage.

■ The Physiology of Stress

The diseases that do us in have changed over the course of history. Bubonic plague killed over a third of the population of Europe in the 14th Century. When Europeans came to the Americas in the 16th Century, they brought diseases to which the native Americans had no immunity.

Large segments of the indigenous population died. As we enter the 21st Century, we have drastically reduced—especially in the developed world—the incidence of bubonic plague, cholera, smallpox, diphtheria, and other infectious diseases. Yet humans today are still subject to premature death; it's just that the death will likely be stress-related instead of caused by bacterial or viral infection. Heart attacks, strokes, ulcers, and colitis: these are the diseases that will most likely kill us or slow us down today. While all of these conditions are the result of complex interactions between genetic predisposition, diet, and lifestyle, they differ from the diseases that laid our ancestors low in that germs are not their primary cause.

Humans have figured out reasonably well how to hold microbes in check, but they still haven't mastered modern stress with a body built for hunting/gathering and farming/herding. Imagine for a moment that you're a primitive cave dweller. You get up one fine day and lumber outside for some fresh air where you are confronted by a saber-toothed tiger. Immediately, your sympathetic nervous system triggers the fight-flight response. Adrenaline is pumped into your blood stream. Blood flows away from your extremities and into your larger muscles. (If the tiger claws your hand or forearm, you will less likely bleed to death.) Your pupils dilate, enabling you quickly to see large, uncomplicated threats (such as charging tigers). Your breathing is rapid and shallow. You are prepared to run from physical danger or confront it with your club. You're in a dangerous situation, but your body is doing everything it can to help you survive.

Now, imagine you're a pre-med student. You walk into your organic chemistry final feeling not too confident. If you bomb this exam, you'll make a C in the class. If you ace it, you'll make an A. The A means med school. The C means selling medical supplies. Your body again springs into action. Blood leaves your extremities. (That's why your hands are cold.) Your pupils dilate, your breathing grows shallow and rapid, and your mind races. The trouble is that your body is preparing you better to face simple, physical threats than the complex, abstract ones which, in fact, populate your universe. You might feel like poking your professor in the nose or running out of the classroom, but fighting or running are much more effective against tigers than against professors.

Unless you learn to respond appropriately to the complexities of modern life, you will not perform as well as you'd like. But that's only a part of the problem. Each time your body prepares you to run from danger or fight it, it is a strain on your body. After the danger passes, the parasympathetic nervous system kicks in and restores your body's equilibrium. But let's suppose that after equilibrium is restored, you are faced with another threat, precipitating another fight-flight response. And about the time that one dies out, another threat comes along, then another. At some point, your parasympathetic nervous system stops restoring your body's equilibrium. You are in a near constant state of vigilance: pumped up, wired, and ready for physical danger. You are also on course for an early heart attack.

All this is to say that it is in your interest to learn to manage stress like a citizen of the 21st Century rather than Og, Son of Fire. If you do, you will perform more effectively in today's rapidly changing, complexity-filled world. You will also do so for a longer period of time. Consider carefully the following tips for managing stress.

Stress Management Checklist

1. Manage you time and organize your things—two sure ways to reduce your headaches and save your stomach lining.
2. DON'T PROCRASTINATE! Do first things first.
3. Don't spread yourself too thin. See number 4.
4. Learn to say "no." See number 2.
5. Cultivate friends as well as contacts.
6. Participate in at least one extracurricular activity because you enjoy it, not because it's going to pay off down the road.
7. Do something fun every day.
8. Exercise regularly. The busier you are, the more important this one is.
9. Eat sensibly.
10. Get enough sleep.
11. Learn to relax. Your college counseling center can teach you Deep Muscle Relaxation and Guided Imagery, but biofeedback, yoga, and meditation are also effective tension reducers for most people.

Read this checklist every day for a week. Read it every week for a month. Read it every month for a year. Repeat as needed.

Recently we heard a psychologist refer to the very competitive university where he worked as a Type-A factory. Type-A individuals are goal directed, driven people who get a lot done, but find it difficult to relax. They are also heart attack prone.

Recent research by health psychologist Margaret Chesney, however, suggested that it is possible to be achievement oriented without the heart attack. The key is in your attitude. Anger and hostility seem to be much more injurious to your heart than ambition and hard work. The most deadly combination of all is the Type A who is unassertive and very angry. This person is too passive to get his/her own way very often, so s/he spends a lot of time feeling frustrated and mad. And because s/he lacks the ability to express himself assertively, s/he has no constructive way of communicating pent-up feelings.

It would appear, then, that you can strive toward your goals if you are flexible about doing so. Frequent frustration and anger are the tip-offs that you are not keeping things in perspective. *If college life seems too hectic, see a counselor.*

In Conclusion, we offer two final bits of advice. Repeat them whenever the stress starts to mount:

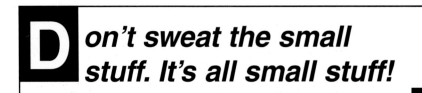

Don't sweat the small stuff. It's all small stuff!

■ Summary

1. Plan a career that interests and challenges you. Money is an important consideration, but not the only one.
2. Don't equate external success with internal fulfillment.
3. Make the principles embodied in the Stress Management Checklist an integral part of your life.
4. The Master Plan is a set of guidelines, not the Ten Commandments.
5. It is not ambition that causes heart attacks, but unbridled ambition.
6. Learn a technique that will enable you to relax during demanding times.
7. If you feel you are under too much stress, get some help. See a counselor.

Name: _____ Date: _____

■ Student Stress Survey

(Circle the number to right of each event you have experienced recently.)

Death of a parent	100	Argument with an instructor	29
Divorce of self or parents	73	Outstanding personal achievement	28
Break-up with boy/girlfriend (relationship > 1 year duration)	65	Boy/girlfriend starts a job	26
		Start school or graduate	26
Arrested and sentenced to jail	63	Move off-campus or dorm reassignment	25
Death of a roommate	63	Lifestyle changes (day to night shift or increase in campus activities, etc.)	24
Death of a close family member	63	
Personal injury or illness	53	Trouble with professor(s)	23
Pregnancy (of self or partner)	50	Withdraw from a class or make an "F"	20
Expelled from school	47	Get a new roommate	20
Get back together with boy/girlfriend	45	Transfer to another college	20
Quit school	45	Change in recreational habits	19
Change in health of family member	44	Change in church/religious activities	19
Move in with boy/girlfriend	40	Change in social activities	18
Sex difficulties	39	Anxious over grade report	18
Gain of a new family member	39	Apply for financial aid	18
Change of major	39	Change in sleeping habits	16
Financial aid for college is withdrawn	38	Can't go home for a special holiday	15
Death of a close friend	37	Change in eating habits	15
Take after-school job	36	Final exams	15
Change in number of arguments with boy/girlfriend	35	Quarter break	13
		Christmas season, Channukah, Ramadan, etc.	12
Sign for school loans	31	
Take > 17 quarter hours of classes	29	Minor violation of law	11
Best friend transfers to another college or leaves school	29		

Add up your score. 150 or less = a 35% chance of serious illness within two years.
A score of 150–300 = a 51% chance of serious illness within two years.
A score of 300 or more = 80% chance of serious illness within two years.

_____

Adapted from Life Events Survey by Holmes and Rahe of University of Washington Medical School.

CHAPTER 10
Finding Work

No student should leave college without career-related work experience. The benefits are simply too great to pass up. Through the right job you can:

- Clarify and validate your career plans
- Make important contacts
- Build skills
- Learn about a company, a field, an industry
- Establish a track record within an organization for whom you might want to work after graduation

You could also collect a pay check, but as important as that is, we believe the above benefits are even greater. So, how do you find the right job, and how do you land it once you find it?

■ Create a Match

You find the right job the same way you choose the right major or plan the right career. You must know yourself well enough to determine if you match the major, career, or job sufficiently to find satisfaction. You must also know enough about the job (or major or career) to make a good decision. And finally, you have to persuade an employer that you match his or her needs. Of course, you first have to find an opening. It all starts with you, however, so that's where we'll begin. All of this is true, moreover, whether you're looking for an internship, part time work to help finance the cost of college, or trying to land a full time position to launch your career after you complete your degree.

The STAR Technique

An essential component of self-understanding is knowing what you can do, what your skills are. Virtually all jobs consist of problems waiting to be solved. You need to show employers how you can solve their problems. If you have the right skills, you will be considered as a serious job candidate. The STAR technique is a method for identifying your skills and communicating them to those in a position to hire you.

Your skills—what you can actually DO for an employer—are potentially your strongest selling points. But don't just list them. Give examples to show how you are skilled at performing a particular task. Be descriptive and use action words. You can strengthen an example by including an outcome. If you quantify the results (e.g., show how you produced a 20 percent increase in output), your example will have even more punch. Sometimes you can't readily quantify results; you have to imply them (e.g., familiarity with different computer languages implies proficiency in them). If possible, include a positive outcome (e.g., successfully implemented new budgeting procedure). Remember, positive results create positive reactions.

Use the STAR (Situation-Action-Result) technique, which is frequently used in personnel work, to communicate your skills with impact. You can use the STAR technique on your resume, in cover letters, and during interviews.

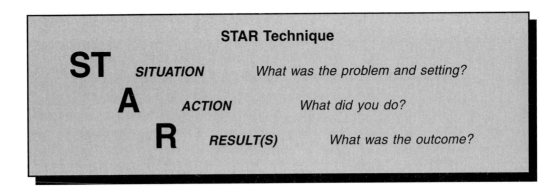

STAR Technique

ST **SITUATION** *What was the problem and setting?*

A **ACTION** *What did you do?*

R **RESULT(S)** *What was the outcome?*

Examples of skills using the STAR technique:

■ Organized Hall Council fundraiser and generated record income.
■ Fluent in French. Conversant in Spanish and German.
■ Wrote award-winning series of articles on alcohol abuse for school paper.
■ Developed new rush strategy resulting in largest pledge class in chapter history.

- Managed MR. TACO fast food restaurant with annual revenue of one million dollars, annual payroll of a quarter million dollars.
- Implemented student-centered teaching to 5th-grade class that resulted in average increase in student achievement-test scores of 17%.
- Handled public relations for benefit concert in Student Center, resulting in first sellout in seven-year history of the event.

Employers have to deal with the real world of limited resources, fierce competition, and the bottom line. They're used to thinking in terms of practical problems, the action taken, and what the consequences are. A salesman takes on a slumping territory, talks to plant managers instead of office managers, and doubles orders in six months. A design engineer introduces computer-assisted design to a project and beats the deadline by two months. A manager introduces an incentive program for her staff, and absenteeism is halved, saving the company $500,000 annually.

Employers want results, preferably quantifiable results. More dollars earned. Fewer hours taken. A greater percent of the market. Better achievement-test scores from students. You probably haven't made anybody megabucks yet, but the same principles apply at any age. A twelve-year-old gets more subscriptions on his paper route than any other carrier and wins a new bike. A high school student organizes a lawn-care business and builds a clientele of twenty-five regular customers. A college freshman makes an A in Computer Science and learns C+ and BASIC. A co-op student assists in developing a system of inventory control that gets the product to the customer three days faster than her company's leading competitor. A fraternity pledge trainer raises the pledges' grades by an average of four-tenths of a point, and for the first time in the organization's history, an entire pledge class is initiated on time.

You can't just tell prospective employers that you have salesmanship, entrepreneurial know-how, computer skills, organizational ability, and leadership (which are the five skills implied in the paragraph above). You've got to show them. The STAR technique enables you to do just that. We believe your skills should be the focus of your entire job-search campaign. You will highlight them on your resume, emphasize them during interviews, mention them in your correspondence.

Achievements on Your Resume

Students sometimes confuse achievements with skills and abilities. You may have been an Eagle Scout, and that's great. But as a line on your resume it doesn't really mean a whole lot. Now tell an employer that: **Managed** a volunteer staff of 14 in the design and construction of a playground for handicapped children, finishing **on-time** and **within budget**. THAT is what an employer wants to see. They want to see those highlighted words that demonstrate specific skills.

Another example of how achievements are confused with skills and abilities is in honorific awards. Great! We're thrilled you were in the National Honor Society, maybe even an officer. But, tell me an achievement. You sell yourself when you use the STAR technique to develop something substantive: As vice-president of National Honor Society, **organized** a fund drive to raise money for the Leukemia Society; **exceeded** our goal by 14%, resulting in special recognition from the Leukemia Society for surpassing our goal. What employer wouldn't like to hire someone who not only makes good grades, but has the skills and abilities to organize and exceed expectations! You get the idea. Now take all those achievements and transform them into skills and abilities using the STAR technique, so that you can wow those potential employers!

Remember, too, the chaotic career paths of the 21st Century will likely require multiple, ongoing, simultaneous job searches. Most of the success stories will be written by hardy, entrepreneurially oriented people who have persuaded lots of others from their extensive network of contacts to purchase their services and products.

The ability to convey your marketable skills concisely, with impact, is itself an impressive skill. It demonstrates self-awareness, analytical ability, organizational skills, and communication skills—a not too shabby list of selling points to have working for you every time you contact an employer.

Once you come up with your marketable skills via the STAR technique, you've completed the most difficult phase of the job search. And since you have identified what you've got going for yourself, you'll also feel like a million dollars. We think that's a pretty good way to start any important endeavor.

■ Finding Openings

There are three principal ways to identify jobs—campus agencies, networking, and the Internet. You can locate openings as a freshman through these means, and you will be able to do so as a graduating senior. I will describe each, but first, let me point out three methods that don't work very well—private employment agencies, the want-ads, and mass mailing your resume.

■ What Doesn't Work

Private Employment Agencies. I wouldn't say that no one ever got a job through one of these operations, but the best candidates do not rely upon them. Yes, there are "Head Hunters" who aggressively recruit experienced managers, executives, and various specialists, but they do not look for college students. Accordingly, you would have to pay an agency for finding you a job. The agency is not interested in your satisfaction, only in getting its fee. Typically, they will pressure you to accept a position you will not like. Some agencies charge the employer instead of the applicant. This is a better route, but their goal is still their fee, not your satisfaction. Nor is their focus on college students. The exception to this rule would be for those with expertise in especially hot fields such as computing, but computer whizzes will probably be able to find a job pretty easily without the assistance of an off-campus employment agency.

The Want Ads. Many jobs are filled with internal candidates and are not advertised. Many of the jobs advertised are filled before they appear in print. They are advertised to "comply" with state and federal regulations. Good jobs typically do not show up in the classifieds.

Mass Mailing Your Resume. Sending out dozens of resumes is costly, time-consuming and ineffective. If you want to reach lots of potential employers, do so over the Internet. Corporations are inundated with unrequested resumes. Unless you send yours to a particular person, it will go to Personnel along with all the others. Instead of distinguishing yourself from the crowd, you've joined it.

■ What Does Work

The Internet. Like most other aspects of our lives, the Internet has changed the way the job search works. Many schools now provide Web sites which enable students to post their resumes. Employers can look at these Web sites for prospective interns, co-ops, and part-time workers. Georgia Tech Career Services uses Interview Track. You can find out more by going to the Career Services web site at http://www.career.gatech.edu/. The Georgia Tech Cooperative Division uses First Place. You can find out more by going to http://www.coop.gatech.edu/welcome2.html.

You can search data bases of employers who hire at your school and send a resume to companies which have an opening. You can also find extensive (probably excessively extensive) resources on careers and job search on the WWW. Search engines like Yahoo and Excite have career-related links, or you can conduct a search by entering "employment" or "jobs." *The Wall Street Journal* recently noted that such a search produced some 2,500 hits!

■ Campus Agencies

Virtually all colleges have career assistance resources. You should take advantage of them **starting as a freshman.** The power of these offices to connect you with actual employers varies widely with the reputation of the school. There are many schools who are not widely known who likely do a very good job of helping students find local jobs because of their strong programs in specialties such as nursing or teaching. More companies recruit at Stanford and MIT, however, than at Northeastern Subnormal.State. Georgia Tech, for example, attracts large numbers of recruiters from many Fortune 500 corporations as well as smaller regional companies. Georgia Tech Freshman can use Career Services to find an internship, a part-time job, or a job on campus. The Cooperative Division will help you to find a position as a co-op. Here are some hints to help you get the best results from your university career services or co-op office:

1. **Sign up early.** Don't wait until the last minute on any aspect of the job search.
2. **Attend the orientation session(s).** Comply fully with the established rules and procedures of the service. If you don't, you may hurt your chances for getting interviews with your preferred companies.
3. **Get a list of which employers will be visiting your campus.** Identify which of those companies you would like to work for. Establish a group of favorite companies and another group of acceptable alternatives.
4. **Prepare your personal resume(s), data sheets, applications, etc. DON'T SKIMP.** Do it right (see Chapter 11).
5. **Take advantage of the seminars and workshops your placement center offers.** Students typically want their college to find them jobs. Often, the career center is best at teaching YOU how to find and land a good job.

There is no standard way for a placement center or co-op office to assign interviews. Some use a lottery. In some centers the companies are given access to student resumes and data sheets. The companies grant interviews only to those students whose records catch their eye. Many companies set GPA cut-offs. They won't look at anybody under a 3.0, a 3.3, or even higher.

If your major is not highly recruited, check with your academic department. Your professors may have some job leads, and in some instances placement may be handled at the departmental level.

As you advance in your college career, it's wise to join a professional association relevant to your professional goals. Sometimes they will have placement services for members. If you need information about such organizations, look in *The Encyclopedia of Associations*, which is found in most main libraries. The Dean of Students office at Georgia Tech lists all campus organizations including professional societies and clubs. Even more important than any formalized placement assistance, professional associations are excellent sources of contacts and information. Which brings us to our final method of finding a job.

■ Networking

John Bolles, in *What Color is Your Parachute?*, says networking is *the* way to fly. He reports an 85 percent success rate. Rather better, wouldn't you say, than the one in 1,499 chance he reports for those who launch a blind resume campaign by mail? Having a good network was an advantage in the Industrial Age. It will be virtually a requirement in the Information Age. When should you start building a network of contacts? NOW! If you feel deficient in this important skill, review "Building Contacts."

Contacts can come from anywhere. Professors and employers are obvious choices, but also consider calling on family connections, friends who have already joined the work force, or alumni from your hometown or from the town where you want to work. If you haven't already done so, join a professional association and start attending their meetings.

Don't wait until you're about to graduate to start organizing your networking efforts. We recommend a 3 x 5 card file system. On the front of each card put the name, address, phone number, and the person's position. (In many cases, you can simply tape the contact's business card to the 3 x 5.) Also indicate your referral source, as that will help you make the proper approach. On the back, put the dates when you met and the nature of the conversation. The important thing is not to follow our system, but that you have a system that works for you—whether it's electronic, loose-leaf, or on a Rolodex™.

This is also a time when it is especially important to keep your calendar up-to-date. Immediately enter the time of every meeting you set—you don't want to miss any. Bear in mind that when you're networking for jobs, you're not actually applying for work. You're trying to find out about your field. You're looking for leads. You're wanting feedback on your qualifications and credentials. Naturally, you wouldn't turn down a good job offer, but networking doesn't usually get you a job by tomorrow or even next week. But if you keep after it for several months, you should have a number of offers to consider. You'll also have contacts who can help you throughout your career.

■ Approaching the Contact

If you write a letter, you can say clearly what needs to be said without distraction. The mail is slower, of course, than the phone, and your letter may be screened. The prospective contact may never lay eyes on it. In any event, you'll probably have to follow up your letter with a phone call to set up a meeting. Increasingly, people are contacted and arrangements made by means of e-mail.

1. *Phone after five. The secretary's having drinks at a fern bar, but the executive is probably still in the office. Maybe he or she will pick up the phone after the twelfth ring.*

2. *Make the secretary your ally. Get her first and last name, and refer to her by her last name. Give her some respect, and she might give you some.*

3. *Don't volunteer information that can be used to screen you out. Be diplomatic but persistent— "Professor Jones referred me to Ms. Jackson, and I really need to speak to her personally."*

4. *If the contact is on another line, say that you'll be glad to hold.*

5. *Generally speaking, it's better to say you'll call back than to leave your name and number. Somehow or other, busy people never seem to return unsolicited phone calls.*

The main difficulty with phoning your contact is getting through. Part of a secretary's job is to protect his or her boss, so you may get put off. Here are some tips to help you reach the contact.

When You Do Get Through

You must be ready. Know what you want. Know what you're going to say. This means thorough preparation before you make the call. We recommend having an outline of your intended comments at hand.

Introduce yourself by giving your name and referral source and stating the purpose of your call. Don't say you're looking for a job. Instead, tell the contact that you're a student at State U., majoring in X, and you'd like to meet to talk about her area. Your experience and coursework have focused on X, but you understand her area (Y) is rapidly expanding, and it's related to yours. Do your best to persuade the contact to meet you. Tell her you want to talk more about particular trends in her area. Identify the trends by name. If she's unwilling to meet with you, get as much information as you can on the telephone. If you keep trying, however, you will eventually find some qualified people who are willing to talk with you in person.

Meeting the Contact

Your purpose for meeting is to get information and advice. Review "Conducting an Informational Interview" in Chapter 6. One of the biggest mistakes you can make during such a meeting is to be vague and unfocused. So prepare thoroughly for the interview by researching the field or industry in question. Complete the self-assessment at the end of this chapter. Have a winning resume in hand (Chapter 11). Develop an "industrial-strength" oral resume. Use the STAR technique to highlight your key strengths.

Preparation is also one of the best antidotes to the jitters, so practice with a friend if you're still feeling nervous. Or talk to a tape recorder or a mirror. To really get a sense of what an informational interview will be like, you can have a friend impersonate the contact and give you some feedback. You can even audio- or video-tape this practice session.

When you finally meet the contact, remind her of your phone conversation and who suggested that you seek her counsel. Describe yourself to her via your oral resume. That will help her advise you according to your specific situation. It's also an opportunity for you to sell yourself. While you didn't come to her for a job, you certainly wouldn't turn the right offer down.

Making an effective oral resume is a skill that you can acquire with practice. It's not easy to give a thumbnail sketch of yourself that says something without it sounding like a canned speech. Try to strike a balance between being overly formal and speaking too conversationally. Try to relax, and remember: you're just one human being trying to tell another who you are so that the other's comments will be pertinent to your situation. You should also know that this is a commonly accepted business practice. It is unlikely that this is the first or last time your contact will hear such a presentation. You'll likely exchange pleasantries for a few minutes, but at some point it will be appropriate to tell your contact about yourself.

In Chapter 5, Janet Smith, freshman, conducted her first informational interview and made her first oral resume. We suggest you review her comments right now. Then take a look at her oral resume as she approaches graduation.

■ Oral Resume of Janet Smith, Senior

"I really appreciate your taking the time to talk with me about current trends in Industrial/Organizational Psychology. Dr. Schwartz said you were doing some really interesting training work with people in sales and middle management. First, let me tell you a little about myself.

"I'm a Psych major, and I'll be graduating at the end of the summer. I should have around a 3.3 grade point average, but I've made all *A*s in my Psych classes except for one *B* in Physiological. I've done an internship at the Acme Company under Dr. Score. Mostly I was involved in test construction. I wrote some of the items, helped with the item analysis, and interviewed most of the subjects.

"The thing was, I gradually realized that the interviewing portion of my job was giving me the most satisfaction. It's not that I didn't enjoy developing the tests themselves. It's just that I preferred having direct contact with people. One of the surveys we developed was designed specifically to assess the morale of people in sales. I could pretty well tell who was going to be successful based on the subjects' scores, but I wasn't supposed to say anything that would influence them. That part frustrated me. I really wanted to use the test results to help these people who were starting out in sales.

"I have done some training work already through my job as an area coordinator with the residence hall program. Before I could start out as a resident assistant, I had to learn basic communication skills and some crisis intervention techniques. This past fall I helped train the new crop of assistants. I consistently got very high ratings, both from the students and from the staff member from housing.

"So what I'm wondering is—How can I break into the training field? And is it possible to do this with only an undergraduate degree? What are my options, and what steps do I need to start taking?"

Basically, you're trying to find out through your questions what this field is like and how you can prepare for it. What specific skills should you try to strengthen? How can you best take advantage of the opportunities available in college to prepare for this field? While it's not appropriate to make a hard sell for yourself, do try to create interest in the mind of the contact whenever possible. For example, if she mentions the need for persuasive skills in her kind of position, recount a situation in which you were persuasive and ask her if that's the sort of ability she has in mind.

Ask her to react to your printed resume (see Chapter 11). What's missing? Is there any fluff that should be trimmed? And take this opportunity to expand your network. Could she suggest others in the field that you could talk with? Does her company offer internship or cooperative positions? Thank her graciously, and offer her a copy of your resume for her files. Then thank her again in a letter.

Before you start arranging meetings with the new contacts she gave you, do some more homework. Revise your resume according to her suggestions. Read up on areas of deficiency that she uncovered. Or get some more training. This is an ongoing process throughout college and throughout your life. After each round of interviews, try to strengthen your suitability for the requirements of the position you're investigating. If you're persistent, you will gradually become a stronger candidate in possession of a winning resume. And at some point you will get interviews for some attractive positions.

■ Conducting an Informational Interview

Dress in appropriate business attire for your interview. Be respectful and use your best manners throughout. Arrive on time and take a small notebook to take notes. Shake hands and introduce yourself with your oral resume. Questions to consider asking:

1. How did you get into this field?
2. What level of education is presently necessary to excel in this field?
3. What does a "normal" work day look like for you?
4. How many hours a week do you normally work?
5. What salary range might an entry level person expect in this field?
6. Is travel a necessary part of this work?
7. What do you like best about your work? Least?
8. What are the most important skills to develop in order to succeed in this line of work?
9. What advice do you have for me as a freshman?
10. Where do you see this field heading in the future?

Send a thank you letter within a week of your interview.

■ Summary

1. Clarifying your goals is an ongoing process.
2. Assess your marketable skills.
3. The STAR Technique is a powerful tool for analyzing your strengths and conveying them to others.

4. The job market of the 21st Century will be competitive and chaotic, so use every resource available to you.

5. The want ads and employment agencies are not generally highly effective avenues to good jobs.

6. The success rates of different college placement centers and Co-op Offices vary widely.

7. Follow your placement center/co-op office's rules exactly to get maximum results.

8. Regardless of the success rate of your campus's career agencies, you should be building a network of contacts which you will maintain and replenish throughout your life.

x9. Start networking only after you've done your homework: self-assessment; a winning resume; preliminary research of field and position.

10. Attend some of the workshops and seminars that your college's career center offers.

CHAPTER 11
Successful Resumes

If a key part of the foundation of your future success is career-related work experience, then a key step in getting it is a good resume. As a freshman, you may have a hard time filling up an entire page without using a 30 point font—a solution not generally favored by employers. In fact, one of the benefits of writing a resume as a freshman is that you will be confronted with your relative inexperience. This should prod you to develop skills, gain experience, and accomplish goals worthy of inclusion on a resume. While you doubtless have much work to do in this vein while you're in college, we've found that most of you already have more going for you than you realize. Another good reason, then, to write a freshman resume is so you'll better realize what you *have* accomplished. Another benefit to writing your resume is that it forces you to get very practical and "real world." Creating the ideal career plan and searching for personal fulfillment are worthwhile pursuits, but don't avoid the concrete and specific task of finding a real job. You'll also find that taking the trouble to create a focused, professional quality resume leads to better self-understanding. And finally, in addition to using your resume for summer jobs, internships, and co-op positions, you'll also find a use for it in scholarship applications and when you seek membership in selective campus organizations.

■ The Impact of the Computer

Computing has changed the way people look for jobs, including how they write their resumes. Resumes are different today for two reasons: 1. The Internet. 2. Scanning Software. While computing has simplified our lives in many ways, it often complicates them as well. You now need two resumes: a generic one for Web sites or your campus's candidate data base and a specific one, targeted for a particular job at a particular company. The two resumes will be similar in many ways, but there should be some important differences. Additionally, you need to consider whether your resume will be scanned because you communicate with a human reader differently than with software.

When you post your resume on a Web site hosted by Career Services or the Cooperative Division, you must create a general picture of your qualifications so as to impress any employer who hires in your field. Should you be invited for an interview, you would want to edit your generic resume so that it more perfectly matches the company in question. Similarly, if you find a suitable job opening through a campus agency, networking, or on the Internet, you would apply to that company with a resume specifically tailored for that company and the job in question, if known. You should still determine whether to write it for human eyes or scanning software.

■ The Resume: Your Personal Ad

Employers are looking for people who will solve their problems. All you have to do is show an employer that you're good at solving his or her kind of problem. Once you've convinced Dynamic Enterprises that you can meet their needs, you've created a match. The resume, by itself, rarely guarantees a job offer. The interview does that. If your resume shows that you match the employer's needs, however, you'll probably be invited to interview. Your resume is a graphic representation of who you are professionally. It's your personal ad.

Having a strong personal ad will be especially important in the volatile job market of the future. The world of work for individuals will be characterized by many jobs, multiple careers, murky career paths, self-employment, and working without a net. Chapter 7 argued that building and maintaining an extensive network of professional contacts will be an essential ongoing part of professional life. You will want many of these contacts to have your resume on file.

■ First Impressions

For employers, the resume is a screening device. Large organizations get hundreds of thousands of them every year. You can pay an employment agency a hundred dollars to come up with a work of art on thirty weight paper, but it's still junk mail to the employee who has to read a hundred of them a day. As we've already suggested, the first "reading" of your resume may be made by a computer rather than a human. Whether it's a person or a PC, you have limited time and space to show that your qualifications differentiate you from the other candidates.

Appearance. Use high quality eight and one-half by eleven inch paper—white, off-white, light gray, or beige. Maybe a designer or entertainer could go with something flashier, but most job seekers are best served by a conservative, professional look. Don't run it off a cheap dot-matrix printer. Use a laser jet or ink jet. Make multiple copies on a high quality copier, using the high quality paper we've already discussed.

Appearance, as well as content, tells the employer a lot about you. Your resume reflects the kind of work you're capable of producing. It should show that you're well organized, that you can communicate clearly, and that you can make a strong visual presentation. The acid test: Does it look good enough for prospective employers to send out as their own work? If it doesn't, it's not good enough.

Use some of the tricks that commercial artists use. When they design ads, they play up important information in the white space, those areas free from text. In poorly constructed resumes we often see dates in those big chunks of white space known as the margin. Dates are not selling points. Instead, use information that does refer to selling points: job titles, degrees, skills, etc.

Stay away from long paragraphs. Your resume should not look like a page out of your American history text. Ads use a few key words, carefully chosen and strategically placed. You further focus attention by using bold print, larger type, bullets, or asterisks. (On a resume which will be scanned, however, you would avoid these graphic tricks because the software might not be able to read them.) Remember, your personal ad must attract attention quickly without appearing garish.

■ Resumes While in School

The principles of creating a winning resume are the same for freshman as they are for graduating seniors or seasoned executives for that matter. In this chapter, we will focus on student resumes because most students enter the job market while they're in college. This can begin your freshman year if you're a co-op student. Part-time work, summer jobs, and internships also may require a resume.

■ Application Form

In most instances you'll have to fill out a standard application or data sheet when applying for a job. We strongly recommend that you supplement it with your own personal resume. Personnel forms are designed to compare all applicants on certain key categories—school, work, etc. It's harder to emphasize your strong points if you don't have top grades or an impressive work history. A personal resume gives you more flexibility. You can highlight whatever you choose. And including a quality personal resume makes you look more professional.

There are a few things that you can do to beef up the form that personnel send you. Usually there will be a place for "Additional Information." Consider listing skills pertinent to the job in question here. (Once more the STAR technique helps you shine.) Try to use every bit of available space to convey pertinent information about you. On the back of some forms there is space for listing coursework and a small "Comments" section. Cite only the most relevant courses and/or those in which you made the best grades. If you write across the page, separating courses with commas, you'll have more room to cover skills and other pertinent information.

Name

Address   City   State   Zip   e-mail   Phone

JOB OBJECTIVE: Most important piece of information on resume; used by employers as screening device or to signal job match; must grab attention and motivate employer to read further. Keep this concise and customized for each use. Must be generic if it goes on a website or data base.

EDUCATION: List in reverse chronological order, putting the most marketable facts—school or degree—first.

Mention any outstanding honors or achievements, such as high GPA, Dean's List.

Give examples of relevant coursework and school-related activities if a recent graduate.

SKILLS:
- Choose skills that are most relevant to job objective.
- Give short statements to support skills.
- Make support statements results-oriented.
- Position most marketable skills first.

EMPLOYMENT: Place strongest of the two sections, employment or education, first.

List in reverse chronological order, putting the most marketable facts—employer or job title—first.

Give functional description of job if employment history is strong and supports job objective.

MISCELLANEOUS:
- Call this section anything applicable—INTEREST ACTIVITIES, ACCOMPLISHMENTS, or ACHIEVEMENTS.
- Give only information that would interest an employer.
- Stay away from personal and chatty information.

REFERENCES: It is assumed you would provide references upon request. Leave this off your resume, unless you're desperately short of items.

REMEMBER: There are no absolute rules in resume preparation. Modify this guide, when necessary, to make the most favorable impression.

■ Name and Address

You want them to remember your name, so you put it at the top of the page. Use a larger font than you use on the rest of your resume. Include your address and a phone number where you can be reached or a message can be left during working hours. Consider buying or sharing an answering machine if you don't have one. Be sure to include your e-mail address.

```
──────────────────────────── EXAMPLE ────────────────────────────

                           Mary Q. Student

Campus Box 007          Georgia Tech Station          Atlanta, GA 30332
                (404) 894-0000     m.student@prism.gatech.edu
```

■ The Job Objective

The job objective is important because it informs the employer if there is a match. The job objective, unlike the rest of the resume, gets close attention on the first pass-through. Therefore, it comes immediately after your name and address at the top of the page. If you're offering what they're seeking, they'll read on.

Create different resumes for different job objectives. If employers don't see a potential match, they might not look further no matter how outstanding your record. Ideally, the job you're looking for is identical to the one they're trying to fill (see JOB OBJECTIVE COMPONENTS chart.)

Avoid platitudes and vagueness. All graduates want "A challenging position with opportunities for advancement." If this is your stated career objective, you've told an employer nothing.

Give any information that will tell the employer where you would fit best. For instance, identify where you want to work in the company (sales, finance, etc.); you may also want to indicate the key skills you have to offer (administrative, quantitative, etc.). Companies don't hire generic employees. They hire researchers, accountants, and personnel directors.

We also advise against listing plural job objectives unless they are closely related. You wouldn't, for instance, say you were looking for an "entry-level position in sales or research" because it makes you look as if you have no clear career goals. If you are looking at rather different positions with different companies, we strongly recommend a different resume highlighting the appropriate skills and experience for each position. This is why having a generic resume on a computer is invaluable. When it comes time to apply for a new job, it is easy to rearrange the material.

Use the actual job titles when you know them—catch the employer's attention right away by showing the possibility of a match. However, don't guess if you're not sure. Personnel may be doing the screening, and they might eliminate you if they don't see what they've been told to look for. If you don't know the exact title, use a standard area such as finance, sales, or research. Everything else on the resume complements the job objective. The education, experience, and skills all show that you can do the job you're trying to get.

Be wary of being too specific when applying for summer jobs, internships, and co-op positions. Many employers don't want to hire someone for a narrowly focused area for two or three months. The exception to this rule is when the work is seasonal or consists of a time-limited project. When stating your job objective for part-time, long-term work, follow the same principles you would when applying for permanent, full-time positions.

If you're applying for a co-op position or an internship, identify the area where you want to work. You probably won't start on anything very high up the ladder. Expect some on-the-job training first.

Sample Student Job Objectives

- Freshman pre-med student seeks summer employment in a hospital.
- Mechanical engineering student seeks internship in automotive manufacturing.
- Management student desires sales position.
- Computer engineering major seeks part-time employment in computer repair.
- Business major desires co-operative placement in marketing.
- International Affairs student desires internship with multinational corporation.
- Internship with emphasis on accounting.
- Summer work in Web site design.

Job Objective Checklist

- Include the exact job title if you know it. Do not guess! The job objective is used as a screening device. If you apply for a job that does not exist, your resume will probably be eliminated before it is read thoroughly. Don't chance it.
- Make the objective meaningful. Everything else in the resume must support and reflect what is said in the objective.
- Be specific and to the point in a targeted resume. Broad objectives are often misinterpreted to be vague and uncertain. Avoid the use of platitudes and cliches. They say nothing and cast doubt on the rest of the resume. You should, however, be more general in a resume that will be posted or included in a data base.
- Include the field you were trained in if this is a selling point. This is especially applicable to those in technical fields.
- Include the functional area of the company where you want to work. Examples of these company divisions are: research and development, production, technical services, information systems/processing, marketing and sales, and administration and finance.
- Include the type of organization (Automotive industry, Aerospace industry, Computer security, etc.) if it is important to you. Keep in mind that this may limit the number of opportunities open to you.

■ Education

List your educational experience in reverse chronological order. If you attend a prestigious school, highlight that fact by using bold face letters or caps. Be sure to include a high GPA and any honors or awards. List the key courses relevant to the job you are seeking. Omit insignificant schooling such as the summer course you took at the junior college back home. Don't mention your high school unless you went to a truly outstanding one or had an especially distinguished record.

EXAMPLE

EDUCATION:

Georgia Institute of Technology   8/2000–Present
B.S.Mechanical Engineering Expected date of graduation: May of 2004
    GPA: 3.1/4.0

Coursework: Calculus, Chemistry, Computer Science

Honors and Activities: Dean's List, Hope Scholar, Freshman Council, Student Society of Mechanical Engineers

---

■ Skills

As we mentioned in Chapter 10, employers want to know what skills you have. You can embed them in your work history, but, if you don't have much experience, you must promote your skills in a section devoted to that purpose. By doing so, you increase your chances of creating a match in the employer's mind. Use the STAR technique we discussed in Chapter 10: Situation, Action, Results. Positive results create positive reactions. And if you can quantify your results, you're talking in a language employers understand.

EXAMPLE

| **Marketing & Sales** | • Grew lawn care business from zero to 17 regular customers in two years. |
| **Organizational Ability** | • Planned campus international festival: designed pamphlets, arranged media events, coordinated work of three committees. |

■ Work Experience

List in reverse chronological order. Play up your work if it's career-related or requires skills you want to emphasize. Whenever possible, use job descriptions that are results-oriented.

Some students find it helpful to have two separate work sections—career-related, which is prominently displayed, and other work, which goes toward the bottom of the page. If you are paying for your own education or a good portion of it, say so. It indicates that you're hardworking and self-sufficient. Even if work is not directly related to your job objective, you often learn skills that are relevant to it. For example, getting customers for a summer lawn care business demonstrates salesmanship. The Chris Shore resume that follows is an example of how a college student can "punch up" his record so it looks more appealing. Chris isn't a stellar student, but he's not a dope either. Chris' GPA is only a 2.9, but a recruiter might still be interested in him because he's got some great work experience. Since he didn't include his GPA, the recruiter will have to meet him and talk to him in person, or over the phone to determine if he's a suitable candidate for the job they have in mind for him. Once Chris gets an interview, he can use his persuasiveness and "can do" attitude to influence the recruiter positively. If you look closely at the paying jobs that Chris has worked, he's really only been a grocery clerk and a sales clerk in a bookstore. However, looking at his resume, he's emphasized many of his skills and abilities acquired since arriving at college. His non-paying internship in a University Press has provided him some excellent experience. You, too, can write a much different resume today than you did right after graduation from high school. Even if you've only been in school one semester, you are now a college student and you have a projected graduation date. You can enhance your resume by including your participation in activities which demonstrate marketable skills. Be sure to ask others to critique your resume and make suggestions. A resume is a living thing that grows as you grow, and changes with your development through your college and life.

EXAMPLE

WORK HISTORY:	**MACY'S DEPARTMENT STORE** Sales Representative 9/98–8/00
Retail Sales	• Created approval displays and set price markdowns which led to **10% increase in departmental sales** for 1999
Communication Skills	• **Explained company procedures** and policies to new company employees during training periods

---

Michael Rod's resume is an example of a student with even less experience. He's been in college a semester and has taken some classes. He is using his collegiate experience along with his high school achievements to sell himself to industry. Note how he puts all of his college-related skills and abilities up-front on his resume. He has a decent GPA as well and includes it for the interviewer's convenience. We have also created a second version of his resume to be suitable for scanning software. These two resumes should give you some ideas about how you can format your own to market yourself for co-op applications, part-time employment, or to apply for a grant, scholarship or fulfill the requirements of this course!

■ Additional Information

An effective job candidate uses every inch of her resume to her advantage. She lists only information that would be a selling point. Most employers don't really need to know that you enjoy swimming and scuba diving. A marine biologist, however, might find it helpful to include these. An engineer cited her plumbing experience when she applied for a position that required wearing a hard hat. She wanted to show that being a woman didn't mean she was afraid to get her hands dirty. One candidate noted that hunting was one of his hobbies. He was applying for a position in a rural area where hunting was extremely popular. By mentioning his interest in guns, he was able to show that he could be one of the boys even though he'd gone to school in the big city. If you can't find another place to include a selling point, stick it in here. Leave it off if it's not relevant. Instead, highlight skills developed through your service within a campus organization, and develop a statement using the STAR technique. If you are asked, then inform the interviewer where you developed the skill.

■ References

Choose them carefully. If you follow the suggestions in this book, you should develop an extensive network of professional contacts. Ask them if they are comfortable writing a favorable recommendation for you. Make sure they have copies of your resume. It will help them to discuss you more knowledgeably when they are contacted by employers. Also, when they see the total package they might be able to come up with other job leads for you. We recommend not listing your references on the resume. It's better to use every precious inch of space to promote yourself.

■ Wording and Phrasing

You control the tone of your resume by the way you write it. There should be no negatives. We remember one student listing a course in which he made a D. In fact, that's about all we can remember. Your resume should be crisp and have punch. Remember, it's your personal ad. Start sentences with verbs or action words, and you'll create the impression that you're a "doer," and not one who sits and waits. Delete pronouns and anything superfluous.

The whole idea is to boil your marketability down to its essence. Recruiters and interviewers, then, will find it easy to remember you and realize why they should hire you. Not every recruiter has been trained by the Department of Human Resources. Frequently corporations send new, inexperienced employees to handle screening interviews at college placement centers. They don't necessarily know how to compare the credentials of the many different candidates. It is to your advantage to make their job easier. A sharp resume is a first step. Make it clear why you're the one their company is looking for.

■ Action Words for Resume Construction

A resume will be the first impression an employer has of you. Make it count! Set the tone by using both action and positive words. Starting sentences with verbs can make your message stronger. Be honest but don't diminish your abilities by using lackluster words.

The following is a list of action words to use in constructing your resume. These are especially useful in a resume which will be read by a person rather than scanned by software. Use verbs (led, accomplished, directed) to communicate to people. Use nouns (Unix, C++, quality control) to communicate to software.

actively	accelerated	accomplished
accurately	achieved	adapted
addressed	adjusted	administered
adopted	advised	analyzed
applies	appointed	appraised
approved	arbitrated	arranged
assembled	assessed	assisted
attentive	audited	authenticated
budgeted	built	calculated
capable	careful	cataloged
certified	chaired	changed
channeled	chiefly	chosen
clarified	coached	collaborated
commended	consistently	constructed
consulted	coordinated	contracted
counsel	created	credited (with)
debated	decided	delegated
delivered	demonstrated	designed
determined	detected	developed
devised	directed	diverted
drafted	drew up	earned
economically	edited	effective
elected	eliminated	enhanced
enthusiastic	erected	established
estimated	evaluated	examined
executive	exhibit	expanded
expedited	experienced	explained
expressed	facilitated	familiar
filed	finalist	finished
forecasted	founded	function
generated	graduated	funded
helped	hired	honored
illustrated	implemented	improved
increased	indexed	influenced
innovation	inspected	installed
instituted	instrumental	integrated
interpreted	interviewed	judged
knowledgeable	launched	lead
lectured	licensed	lobbied
logical	maintained	major
managed	manufactured	marked
maximum	measurable	mediation
merchandised	merit	methodically

minimal	moderated	modified
most	motivated	motorized
narrated	navigated	negotiated
obtained	organized	originated
overcame	participated	perceptive
performed	persuaded	pinpointed
planned	positive	prepared
presented	primary	principal
produced	proficient	programmed
progressed	projected	promoted
proposed	proved	provided
publicized	qualified	quoted
recommended	recorded	reduced (losses)
reinforced	renovated	reorganized
reported	represented	researched
resolved	responsible	responsibilities
restored	revamped	revenue
revised	reviewed	satisfactorily
saved	scheduled	schematic
selected	served	significantly
simplified	sold	solved
solution	specialized	spoke
stabilized	strategy	streamlined
structured	successfully	suggested
summarized	supervised	supplemented
supported	surveyed	systematized
taught	trained	upgrade
wrote		

■ Types of Resumes

Chronological

This is the most traditional type—which is its advantage. Employers are familiar with it. The disadvantage of the chronological resume is that it plays up your work history even if it's sketchy or unrelated to your job objective. If you follow the Master Plan outlined in this book, you will develop a solid work history. As a freshman, however, your professional history is probably weak. If so, consider another type of resume. If you want to see an example of a rather ho-hum, but nevertheless, chronological resume, look at Malik Franklin's resume, which appears at the end of this chapter. The same information is rearranged and reworked in the next resume example to become a great example of another type of resume: a functional resume. A chronological resume can be made to look more attractive than what we've done here, and for some people a chronological resume is the right way to go. We wanted to illustrate how using white space, bullets, bold face, and organization can strengthen appearance. The blandness of the first resume is not related to the fact that it's chronological at all—the reason it's ho-hum has to do

―――――― EXAMPLE OF A STUDENT RESUME ――――――

CHRIS SHORE

Box 599 Holcomb, University of Arkansas, Fayetteville, AR 72701
e-mail-chris.shore@ARKU.edu

JOB OBJECTIVE: Summer internship with a **daily newspaper.**

EDUCATION

- **UNIVERSITY OF ARKANSAS**

  Journalism Major
  Anticipated Graduation: December, 2002

- **FAYETTEVILLE HIGH SCHOOL**

  Graduated June, 1998

CAREER-RELATED EXPERIENCE

UNIVERSITY OF ARKANSAS PRESS   Sept. 1999–Present

- Assistant, Promotion and Marketing
  In charge of **promotion** for *VINEGAR DAYS*, by Max Middlesex

- Intern
  Wrote jacket copy and designed advertising layouts for national authors; collaborated on coordinating autographings; ACCOMPLISHMENT: Consistently high appraisals resulted in promotion to salaried position.

SKILLS

- **EDITING & PUBLISHING:** Currently being trained in **manuscript and newspaper editing** by University of Arkansas Press; editor of high school newspaper; **ACCOMPLISHMENT:** Received **superior rating** from Arkansas High School Press Association for editorial on possible teacher strike.

- **INTERVIEWING: Feature editor** and **reporter** for high school newspaper; **ACCOMPLISHMENT**: Received **superior rating** from Arkansas High School Press Association for interview with city government leader.

- **LEADERSHIP:** Participated in "CLOSE-UP" political awareness program for a week in Washington, DC; Student Body President, Alday Junior High School.

- **PRODUCTION:** Experienced in all phases of publication production, including copy preparation, design, typesetting and keylining.

ADDITIONAL WORK HISTORY

- Grocery Clerk   IGA   Summer 1996
- Sales Clerk   Barnes & Noble   Summer 1997
- Grocery Clerk   IGA   Summer 1998

─── EXAMPLE OF A STUDENT RESUME ───

Michael Rod

Campus: Georgia Tech Box 57123   **Home: 7110 Maple Street**
e-mail: gt9987b@prism.gatech.edu

Atlanta, GA 30332   **Columbia, SC 29223**
(404) 676-6923   **(803) 788-1234**

JOB OBJECTIVE   **Electrical Engineering major seeking co-operative placement in research and development.**

EDUCATION

GEORGIA INSTITUTE OF TECHNOLOGY	**8/99–present**
Freshman	**GPA: 3.4/4.0**

Electrical Engineering
- **Vector Calculus**
- **Computer and Digital Design Fundamentals**

RICHLAND NORTHEAST HIGH SCHOOL	**1995–1999**
	GPA: 4.4/4.0

Advanced Curriculum
- Derivative and Integral Calculus
- Advanced Physics
- Advanced English and American History
- National Honor Society

Related Activities and Awards
- Junior Engineering Technical Society
- Engineering Explorers
- Richland Northeast Senior Achievement Award in Science

PEOPLE SKILLS

Developed strong leadership and communications skills through the following:

- Palmetto Boys State
- Member, Richland Northeast H.S. Band
- Student Government
- Church youth group

EMPLOYMENT

- Waiter, Quality Inn, May–August, 1999
- Busboy, Quality Inn, January–May, 1999
- Busboy, Collaro's Italian Restaurant, Summer 1998
- Assistant Plater, Davis & Rodgers Plating, Summer 1997

SCANNABLE VERSION OF MICHAEL ROD'S RESUME

Michael Rod

Campus: Georgia Tech Box 57123   Home: 7110 Maple Street
e-mail gt1234a@prism.gatech.edu

Atlanta, GA 30332   Columbia, SC 29223
(404) 676-6923   (803) 788-1234

JOB OBJECTIVE   Electrical Engineering major seeking co-operative placement in research

and development.

EDUCATION

GEORGIA INSTITUTE OF TECHNOLOGY	8/99–present
Freshman	GPA: 3.4/4.0

Vector Calculus

Electrical Engineering

Computer and Digital Design Fundamentals

RICHLAND NORTHEAST HIGH SCHOOL	1995–1999
	GPA: 4.4/4.0

Advanced Curriculum
Derivative and Integral Calculus
Advanced Physics
Advanced English and American History
National Honor Society

Related Activities and Awards
Junior Engineering Technical Society
Engineering Explorers
Richland Northeast Senior Achievement Award in Science

PEOPLE SKILLS

Developed strong leadership and communications skills through the following:
Palmetto Boys State
Member, Richland Northeast H.S. Band
Student Government
Church youth group

EMPLOYMENT
Waiter, Quality Inn, May–August, 1999
Busboy, Quality Inn, January–May, 1999
Busboy, Collaro's Italian Restaurant, Summer 1998
Assistant Plater, Davis & Rodgers Plating, Summer 1997

EXAMPLE OF A STUDENT RESUME

NICHOLAS BENNINGS

Campus: 37-G Addison Hall, Bates College, Lewiston, ME
Permanent: 1301 DALRYMPLE, Hartford, CT 06110, 203/299-4636
e-mail—Nbennings@aol.com

JOB OBJECTIVE: Seek internship or summer employment with a **metropolitan museum**.

EDUCATION:

	BATES COLLEGE	GPA: 3.7/4.0 1998–Present

**Anthropology
Major**

- Social Anthropology
- Cultural Anthropology
- Greek and Roman Art and Architecture
- Art of the Middle Ages
- Dean's List first semester
- Member, The Arts Society

	MERRIMAC HIGH SCHOOL	GPA: 3.5/4.0

**Advanced
Curriculum**

- Advanced English and social sciences
- President, Art Club
- National Honor Society member

EXPERIENCE:

	VANDERNESSEN MUSEUM OF FINE ARTS	Summer 1998

Volunteer

- Worked with curator to set up museum exhibits
- Prepared art objects for shipment

	FUN WORLD AMUSEMENT PARK	Summer 1997

Games Host

- Developed strong **communication** and **public relations skills** through heavy customer contact with the lack of white space and the fact that the information is in paragraph form (the reader has to work to get the information) and there are no enhancements through the use of typing elements.

Functional

Since work is played down, you can emphasize the skills necessary to perform the job you're seeking. And since you're not following any prescribed order, you can position the most relevant skills and experiences higher on the page. Its main disadvantage is that employers see fewer of this type, and that might bother some of them. Of course, it might also catch their eye. Look at the second resume of Malik Franklin. Note how layout and emphasis on skills have completely changed the appearance of Malik. The reader, likewise, does not have to work very hard to determine what he's been doing and where he's gotten his experience and what his experience is in. By investing some time and energy in to formatting and enhancing the appearance with typing elements and white space, Malik looks like a much more attractive candidate. Investing a little time to make your resume the best introduction possible is well worth the time.

Cover Letters that Work

Cover letters should be strong enough to stand on their own and promote you even when separated from your other credentials. In other words, no "Dear Mr. Gronk, I'm interested in working for your organization. Enclosed, please find my resume. Sincerely . . . "

Use the cover letter to elaborate on any information that is briefly covered in the resume and is a selling point. Use key phrases taken from your resume. Advertising relies on repeated presentations, and you're advertising yourself. We all know "Just Do It," promotes NIKE because you've seen the commercial countless times.

Format

The opening paragraph needs to serve as a "hook." It should motivate employers to read further. Mentioning something interesting about the company (not just something found in the yellow pages) shows that you believe their company is worth spending time on. Like the resume, the cover letter needs to show how a candidate's skills meet the employer's needs. State specifically how you can help solve the employer's problems. Indicate why you're contacting the employer and how you found out about the job (magazine article, newspaper ad, professional contact, etc.).

You can usually find ample information on a company's Web site. If you need additional information, the library will have sources such as the *Business Periodical Index, Reader's Guide, Moody's Index,* and *Dun's Career Guide.* Career Services can also help you find such information. You want to be able to say specifically why you're interested in the particular organization you're contacting.

Body of Letter

Present your case as a strong candidate. Briefly cite whichever of your academic achievements, skills, accomplishments, and work history are relevant. Give specific examples with details. Repeat some of the key phrases contained in your resume to reinforce your selling points. Tell them what your main selling points are. Mention enclosing a resume for their convenience.

Closing Paragraph

Ask for action. Be confident and assertive about doing so. You wouldn't apply for the job if you didn't think you were the right one to do it. State that you will contact them in ten days to two weeks. *And do it.* Note how Nicholas Bennings's cover letter complements his resume. Either letter or resume can stand alone, but together they build an even stronger case for the candidate.

—————————— EXAMPLE OF A COVER LETTER ——————————

February 2, 2000

Museum of Natural Artifacts
    and History
1748 Lincoln Square
New York, NY 10025

Attn: Mr. Carson Donnelly,
       Director of Student Internship Programs

Dear Mr. Donnelly:

I am interested in applying for a summer internship offered through the Museum of Natural Artifacts and History. *American Historian* magazine recently reported that the MNAH provided the "most extensive training—outside of a dig—to those students interested in archaeology and anthropology." Although you have twenty-five summer internships, it's obvious that you have to be selective in choosing participants. Here's why I can make a positive contribution.

First, I have prior experience working in a museum. While in high school I was a volunteer at the Vandernessen Museum of Fine Arts. There I helped the curator set up exhibits and prepare art objects for shipment. One project that I particularly enjoyed working on included over 250 Native American artifacts and featured a full-scale replica of a wigwam.

Second, my academic accomplishments include a GPA of 3.7 after one semester as an anthropology major at Bates College and membership in the National Honor Society.

Finally, I have strong communication and leadership skills. I have proven experience in leading groups, being a team member, and working with the public, all assets that are helpful in a museum environment.

I have enclosed a resume for your convenience. I am eager to discuss internship opportunities and will contact you in three weeks to arrange for an interview.

Sincerely,

Nicholas Bennings
37-G Addison Hall
Bates College
Lewiston, ME 04240

Optically Scannable Resumes

Many large and mid-sized companies are automating their hiring processes. The use of resume scanning software is increasing and changing the way resumes are written. Including "key words" for your profession may be critical to your resume being selected in a job search. The following rules should be followed when sending your resume to larger companies or companies that you know use optical scanners to review resumes. Electronic Resume Revolution *by Joyce Lain Kennedy is an excellent reference on this subject.*

■ *Use white or light beige standard 8.5" x 11" paper. Avoid colored or textured papers.*

■ *Avoid graphics, shading, italic text, underlining, script, vertical lines, parentheses, brackets, leader dots.*

■ *Use sans serif fonts, i.e., Helvetica, Futura, Universe, Optima, ITC Avante Garde Gothic or very popular serif fonts, i.e., Times, New Century Schoolbook, Palatino, ITC Bookman, or Courier. Do not use decorative typefaces or fonts.*

■ *Use horizontal lines sparingly, always leave at least 1/4-inch of white space around them.*

■ *Use industry jargon and abbreviations, i.e., CAD, ISO, Unix, MBO, TQM.*

■ *Use general abbreviations sparingly. It's best to spell it out.*

■ *A laser printer is best.*

■ *Your name should be the first line of your resume. If a third party is forwarding your resume, their name or sticker should be at the bottom of your resume.*

■ *When faxing your resume, set fax machine to "fine mode."*

■ *Always send originals.*

From the 1994–95 Career Guide, Georgia Institute of Technology

Malik Franklin

1423 33rd Street, NW
Vincent, Ohio 44646
216/833-5531 (home)
404/894-1111 (school)
gt4312b@prism.gatech.edu

EDUCATION: Attended the Georgia Institute of Technology from September 1996 to May 2000. Will graduate with a Bachelor of Science degree in Management in June. Took many finance and management classes.

Honors & Activities: Lettered 4 years and started 2 years in a major college football program. Dean's List, 2 times. Elected team captain for various games at Georgia Tech. Served as coach for church league basketball team and junior high football and basketball teams. Active in Boy Scouts and Boy's Clubs of America.

WORK HISTORY:

Summer 1996 CLEANER'S HANGER COMPANY, Mendosa, Ohio, Assistant. Responsible for working with different groups in production and administration. Duties included: assisting in the repair and maintenance of production equipment and the facilities, filling purchase orders, assisting the managers behind the counter, and making deliveries.

Winters 1996–98 HOLY INNOCENCE CHURCH, Atlanta, Georgia, Office Staff/ Coach. Responsible for scheduling referees for games, keeping payroll records, and answering questions concerning the church's basketball league.

SKILLS & HOBBIES: Familiar with Word, Excel, PowerPoint, Lotus, dBase III, and BASIC. Enjoy swimming, jogging, and reading.

References Furnished Upon Request

MALIK FRANKLIN

1423 33rd St., NW/Vincent, Ohio 44646   216/833-5531 (home)   404/894-1111 (school)
gt4312b@prism.gatech.edu

OBJECTIVE

A management position in the banking industry involving commercial loans and/or bonds and securities.

EDUCATION

GEORGIA INSTITUTE OF TECHNOLOGY   **May 2000**
  B.S. Management

Major Coursework:

- Commercial Bank Management
- Real Estate Investments
- Organizational Structure Design
- Economic Theory of the Firm

- Investments
- Accounting
- Finance
- Personnel Management

QUALIFICATIONS

Portfolio Management: Successfully assembled and managed stock portfolio for investments class project. Received a 300% increase in revenues at end of term.

Bank Management: Analyzed a bank's financial position and made effective recommendations to top management for class project. Bank's return on equity increased 6%.

Leadership: Provided leadership and guidance through various activities, including Boy Scouts, coaching, church league basketball, and Boys' Clubs of America.

Computer Skills: Competent in Lotus, dBase III, BASIC, HTML, Java, and MicroSoft Office.

WORK HISTORY

Cleaner's Hanger Company, Mendosa, Ohio   Summer 1998
  Filled purchase orders and maintained facilities.

Holy Innocence Church, Atlanta, Georgia   Winters 1998–2000
  Coordinated referee schedules and kept records of payrolls
  for church basketball league.

ACCOMPLISHMENTS

- Provided 100% of college expenses and contributed to family support through athletic scholarship and summer employment.
- Lettered 4 years and started 2 years in major college football.
- Dean's List
- Elected team captain for three games at Georgia Tech.

■ Resume Checklist

Did You?	Yes	No
1. Prominently display your name?	_____	_____
2. Put in a complete address and zip code?	_____	_____
3. List e-mail address?	_____	_____
4. List day-time telephone number and area code?	_____	_____
5. Specify job objective?	_____	_____
6. Describe your education?	_____	_____
7. Complete a work experience section?	_____	_____
8. Include skills using STAR Technique?	_____	_____
9. Include information on affiliations and activities?	_____	_____
10. Use words that are positive and action oriented?	_____	_____
11. Check names and dates for accuracy?	_____	_____
12. Verify technical terms and descriptions?	_____	_____
13. Check for grammatical errors and typos?	_____	_____
14. Shorten or tighten sentences?	_____	_____
15. Use white space to advantage?	_____	_____
16. Use bullets and bold face to advantage?	_____	_____

For Scannable Resumes

	Yes	No
17. Eliminate bullets, lines, and bold face?	_____	_____
18. Emphasize nouns rather than verbs?	_____	_____

Name

Address _____ City _____ State _____ Zip _____

e-mail _____ Phone _____

Job Objective:

Education:

Skills:

Employment:

Activities:

CHAPTER 12
Effective Interviewing

Image © PhotoDisc, Inc., 1996.

Some years ago, a savvy corporate recruiter began an address to a group of college seniors by asking how many of them were going into sales. Only a few of the several hundred in attendance raised their hands. The speaker smiled and corrected his audience. "Most of you are wrong. You're ALL going into sales. Every time you look for a job, you've got to sell yourself." We would add that you must also be a salesperson when you try to get your idea across at a meeting, win a debate or election, or convince your friends or colleagues to volunteer for your project.

While communicating effectively is important in any setting, mastering the job interview itself is an invaluable skill to acquire. Bear in mind that most of the principles involved in interviewing for a job are transferable to applying for ANY position: being selected for Freshman Council, becoming an officer in your fraternity/sorority, or getting an internship. The rest of the chapter will focus on this crucial skill. Happily, it is possible to summarize the essence of effective interviewing in one sentence:

Convince the employer that you match that employer's needs.

This isn't always easy, but it should help you make sense of the "interview game." Moreover, this it is the same objective behind your resume, your cover letter, and all of your communication with employers.

■ Preparation Is Key

Good coaches never brings a team out on the field without first preparing the players for the game. They need to know who they're up against, what to expect, and how to score points. Otherwise, they might as well stay in the locker room.

It's the same with interviewing. The more you know about the company, the questions they'll ask, and how to sell yourself, the better your chances for getting an offer. There are five steps to take.

Interviewing Game Plan

Before the Interview

1. Conduct a thorough self-assessment (goals, experience and skills).

2. Develop a good resume.

3. Research the company and industry.

4. Be familiar with typical questions and develop effective answers.

5. Dress appropriately.

During the Interview

1. Show enthusiasm.

2. Emphasize your selling points.

3. Sell yourself as a match.

4. Ask intelligent questions.

After the Interview

1. Process the interview and determine next steps.

2. Send a thank you letter.

1. Conduct a thorough self-assesment.
Before you can get anywhere in finding a job, you need to know yourself—where you've been, where you're headed, and what you're good at. This may seem elementary, but when an interviewer says, "Tell me about yourself," you should be able to state your goals, experience, and skills.

2. Write a strong resume.
By now you should have a winning resume. If you haven't, go back to Chapter 11 and pull one together. Make sure that your references have copies of your resume. It could be embarrassing for both of you if they have to "wing it" when employers call them. Besides, they might not remember all your shining qualities without a little prompting.

3. Research the company thoroughly.
You can't make a strong case for being hired if you don't know anything about them. How does an employer know you'll be a help if you can't show you understand their needs? And just as important, how do you know they're the right company for you? As an intern, you may spend several months working with a company. As a co-op, several years. That's a substantial commitment to rush into blindly, so find out what you can about a prospective employer.

There is ample information available about the corporate world. You'll have to dig a little harder to find out about other employers—schools, hospitals, and small businesses, but the same principals apply in each case. The more you know about a prospective employer, the better off you are.

Categories to Consider when Researching a Company

- ■ What the company does: Sell a product or a service? How diversified is its line? A multinational corporation may have hundreds. A small private school, just one.
- ■ The stability of the organization: What is the outlook of the industry and the particular company? How big were sales last year? Is the company growing? Who are the competitors? What about the company's reputation? Are there plans for new products or divisions? The idea is to avoid climbing aboard a sinking ship. Or better yet, to get in just before the company takes off.
- ■ How the company operates: What is its organizational structure? Are there many levels of employees or just a few? Is it publicly owned, a Mom and Pop store, or a governmental agency? How large? Where located? More than one location? What is management like? How old? How qualified? How did they get there? Are there training programs for employees? What is the typical path for someone with your career objective? How are the employees treated? What about salaries? Benefits? Is there a recognizable corporate philosophy?

Sources of Information about a Company

The Internet. All large organizations and most small ones provide information through a Web site. At a minimum, you should check out an organization's home page before talking with them or working a career fair. In fact, it's easier than ever to do research through the Internet. A small organization might not be able to afford an expensive brochure, but they can put up a Web site.

Networking. As mentioned earlier, it is easier to research a multinational corporation than the corner drugstore. Perhaps it would be more accurate to say that you have to rely on different sources to investigate a small organization. Generally speaking, you will have to rely on word of mouth. If you're intent on building success, however, you will aggressively cultivate sources of information through networking. Touch as many bases as you can, and see what you can find out.

Here are some other tips when researching a smaller organization:

- ■ Talk with other students. Who else has interned for this company or taken a co-op position with them? What was their experience like? This sort of insider information is invaluable.
- ■ Check with professional associations. Is the prospective employer a member? In good standing? Chambers of Commerce, Better Business Bureaus, and Speakers' Bureaus can all provide a few basic facts. In a very small community, the office of the mayor or city manager may serve as a primary source of information. Local newspapers and periodicals are another important source. If you have the gumption to do it, visit a local bar, diner, or restaurant that serves employees or clientele. Strike up a conversation, and see what you can find out.
- ■ A pre-med student applying for a position at a hospital would want to take a look at the hospital's brochure, find out about the demographics of the clientele, and get information from the local medical society. Finally, a really proactive student might visit with staff members in the hospital cafeteria or snack bar and pump them for information.

Our university recently interviewed candidates for an important administrative position. All the candidates were highly qualified and had impressive resumes. We arranged for all of them to speak with a variety of students and staffers. One of them took an extra step by walking back to the campus on his own to eat in the student cafeteria, wander the grounds, and chat with whomever he bumped into. For his efforts, he learned a lot about us. We also learned something important about him and his interest in the job.

If you're unable to find much information about the particular company you're considering, be sure to research current trends in your field. Your academic department may have some information about your field of interest. Also, consider going to the library and checking out a few of the relevant trade journals. Professional societies often have Web sites which are very informative. Having such up-to-date knowledge will help you to ask the key questions to see how an organization measures. You'll also come across much more impressively during the interview.

Preparing to Enter the Full-Time Work Force

While you might not want to commit the time to thoroughly investigate a company for whom you're considering only part-time work, you will eventually graduate. The stakes will be higher and knowing what you're getting into when you sign on for an entry level job will be more important than ever. If, at that time, you are researching a large corporation, ask for assistance at the library. Research librarians can provide you with a wealth of material on products, services, and key personnel Some basic sources to investigate include:

Annual Reports. Every publicly held business is required to publish an annual report. You can get a copy from the firm's public relations department of often from placement offices, career planning centers, stock brokerage firms, public libraries, etc. It typically contains:

> Statement from president
> Current activities and future plans
> Summary of sales and profits
> Independently audited financial statements
> Comparison of this year's earnings to last

Employment Brochures. Organizations which employ several hundred people usually publish employment (recruiting) brochures. These are available through the campus placement offices and college libraries. Or you can directly contact the company's college relations or personnel department. These brochures are a good source of information on the corporate environment. Pictures and quotes give you clues about the company's management style.

Investment Reports. Many investment firms make an analysis of public business firms whose stock is available for purchase. These reports may include such information as sales volume, earnings, and current market demand for products. Sources for stock market reports include *Value Line Investment Surveys, Standard and Poor's Stock Reports,* and *Moody's.* You could also contact a brokerage house as a potential client and get information.

Product Information. To learn about the range of products that a particular company manufactures, consult the *Thomas Register,* and eighteen-volume annual publication. Volumes 1–10 are like the yellow pages: under each product category, all manufacturers are listed alphabetically and geographically. Volumes 11–12 name all products made by each company. Volumes 13–18 contain sample pages from company catalogs. You can also get product information from trade magazine ads or from product brochures put out by the company.

Business Periodicals. These are good sources of information about corporate environment and current happenings. Features on top executives give you a feel for the management philosophy of a company. To find magazine articles look under the *Business Periodical Index* and *Reader's Guide to Periodical Literature.* Other sources to consider would include: *The Wall Street Journal, Fortune, Forbes, Barron's, Financial World, Business Week,* etc.

4. Be familiar with typical questions and develop effective answers. It is common for students to look over a professor's old exam questions as they prepare for finals. Why would you want to do any less in preparing for an interview? Randall Powell in *Career Planning Today* says that interviewers want the answer to four questions:

- What are your qualifications?
- Do your qualifications match our needs?
- Why are you interested in our company?
- Are you the best person for the job?

To get answers to these questions, they'll probe your background with other additional questions. Some may seem unrelated or vague. Some might make you sweat. But unless the interviewer is a rookie or a real sadist, her questions have a purpose. She's trying to find out if you're the right person for the job.

The questions can be open-ended: "Tell me about yourself." They can be very specific: "Explain why your grades are low." We've included a list of the most commonly asked questions. FAMILIARIZE YOURSELF WITH THEM, AND DEVELOP SOLID RESPONSES TO EACH ONE.

When the competition for a particular job or company is especially stiff, recruiters can ask some questions about how you've handled challenges:

- Tell me about a difficult problem you've faced and how you handled it.
- Tell me about your biggest challenge as a student (a sorority officer, an employee at a fast food restaurant, etc.) and how you handled it.
- Tell me about a setback you've faced and what you learned from it.

Have answers ready for these questions. And remember, when Ms. Manager says, "Tell me about yourself," she doesn't really want to know who you had a crush on in sixth grade or why you think hang gliding is totally awesome. She wants to know about your achievements, your career goals, and why you chose your major. The bottom line is always: Can you meet the needs of our company?

The STAR technique (Situation-Action-Results) is a powerful way for you to show her that you can. See Chapter 10 if you need a quick refresher. Armed with a list of your skills in academic, extracurricular, and work situations you can face even the toughest questions. The STAR technique is especially helpful in fielding open-ended questions (Tell me about your extracurricular activities) and handling stress questions (Why should I hire you?). You can also use it to keep an unfocused interviewer on track.

Outline responses to difficult or complicated questions. When discussing your weaknesses, make sure your response doesn't conclude with a statement that leaves a negative impression. Counter the negative by adding something positive:

> *My GPA is lower than I would like because I had to work twenty hours a week to put myself through school. I was still able to graduate in four years, and I feel I learned a lot on the job.*

Or:

> *I wasn't sure of my major when I started school, and my grades reflected that. Once I settled on civil engineering, my grades improved.*

Questions You'll Want to Ask

Your questions are important, too. Remember, you're also evaluating them. Can they meet your needs? Besides, what you ask says something about you—your enthusiasm, your maturity, your understanding of the problems facing your field. Never ask obvious ques-

---

Questions Interviewers Ask

Tell me about yourself.

Why do you feel qualified for this position?

What would you consider an ideal job?

What do you know about our company?

What are your short-term goals? Your long-term goals?

What are your strengths? Your weaknesses?

What have been your most satisfying and disappointing experiences?

Why did you major in _____?

Which courses did you like best?

Explain why your grades are low.

How did you finance your education?

Do you plan to continue your education?

What did you learn from your work experience? From school?

What managerial or leadership positions have you held?

Why did you leave your job(s)?

Tell me about your extracurricular activities.

What was the last book you read?

Where would you like to work? (geographic area)

Are there any places you wouldn't want to work?

How do you feel about putting in overtime?

---

tions, ones that could be answered by reading the company brochure. Also, steer away from questions about salary, vacation, and company benefits during an initial contact—that is, unless the interviewer brings them up.

Be sure to ask specific questions about the job as it relates to your background. For instance, ask about the hardware and software used if you're a computer programmer. Ask about laboratory equipment if you're a medical technician. A coach might want to know about practice facilities and the equipment budget.

5. Dress Appropriately.

First impressions may be superficial, but they matter. You must do your homework to know what appropriate dress is for a particular company. Many high-tech companies embrace the most casual of dress codes. Jeans and sweatshirts are OK. There are still plenty of places, however, that expect a suit and tie for men and professional business attire for women. Know what to expect before the interview. Err on the cautious side if you're not sure—which is to say dress up. Your Career Services office probably has a tip sheet on what to wear. One safe course of action to follow is to dress the way successful people in the field you're entering dress. Neat, clean, and currently stylish is what you should aim for. Depending upon your professional ambitions, now may be a good time to invest in a decent suit and a good pair of dress shoes.

During the Interview

1. Be confident and positive. All employers want someone who is self-assured and able to perform under pressure. Try to look at each interview as an opportunity to demonstrate that you're that kind of person. Solid preparation for the interview is a great way to gain confidence. Arrive a few minutes early. You'll have the time to check your appearance, review your resume, and collect your thoughts.

When you first meet Mr. or Ms. Manager, make eye contact and shake his/her hand when (s)he offers it. Some male interviewers are unsure of protocol and may not extend a hand to a female candidate. We suggest that she offer him her hand as an icebreaker. Once the interview starts, be positive about yourself and the company you're applying to work for. The person who interviews you is committed to that company. If you seem apathetic or indifferent to the company, you are, in effect, rejecting the interviewer.

Wait until the interviewer indicates for you to take a seat. If she obviously stalls about asking—a technique sometimes used in stress interviews—announce to her that you'll sit and wait until she's ready to begin. If you have the opportunity, take a look around the office before the interview starts in earnest. If the room has family pictures and other homey touches, you're probably dealing with a people person. An impersonal atmosphere tips you off that ideas are this interviewer's preference.

Each interviewer will have his or her own style, but all interviews can be categorized on two dimensions: **Structure** and **Focus**.

High Structure: Interviews are standardized. The same questions are asked each candidate and scored on the same scale.

Low Structure: Interviews are NOT standardized. Different questions may be asked of different candidates. This is a more intuitive approach.

Experience-based Questions: The interviewer asks the candidates what they have actually done in the past. "Tell me about a time when . . . "

Situational Questions: The focus is on hypothetical situations. "What would you do if . . . "

The interview method preferred by most professionals today is the Structured/Experienced-based interview. Past experiences can come from a variety of areas (in order of preference):

- Job experiences (including co-op and internships)
- College experiences (e.g., classes, frats/sororities, groups, sports)
- High school experiences (e.g., classes, groups, science fairs, sports)
- Volunteer experiences (e.g., Scouts, Habitat for Humanity, Tutoring)
- Family experiences
- Peer experiences

Research indicates that the six most popular characteristics which interviewers probe are the following:

- Achievement
- Conscientiousness
- Teamwork
- Communication
- Leadership
- Problem Solving

We recommend that you develop good answers to a structured/experienced-based interview question regarding each of these characteristics. This may seem a bit daunting, but try to look at a tough interview as a challenge and an opportunity. If you've taken the trouble to prepare, the interview will only make you look stronger than the others. It's a good idea to rehearse with friends, especially if you anticipate a tough interview. Make a game of it. See how impossible you can be with each other. The real interview will seem like a piece of cake in comparison. Third, get some current information on interviewing by visiting your Career Services office or Web site.

2. Emphasize Your Selling Points. Go into each interview with a mental list of your selling points—the skills and experiences that qualify you for this particular job. *Make sure you discuss each one before the end of the interview.* This is the single most important step in the entire interview. If you run into an inexperienced or unfocused interviewer, be tactfully assertive and take the lead yourself. Here are some suggestions:

That's interesting. Maybe we can talk about that more after the interview.

What you're saying reminds me of _____. Let me tell you what I did.

I've had a similar experience which really tested my _____ skills. Let me tell you about it.

3. Sell Yourself as a Match. Not only must you emphasize your selling points, but you must also establish a bridge between your skills and the company's needs. This means that you will highlight some of your qualifications more than others. Specifically, you should dwell on those of your selling points that are most crucial to the performance of the job you are applying for. If you are a freshman, most companies are looking for a

> *"Knowing how to interview is so important. If you want a job, you either have to have a 4.0, lots of work experience, or be able to interview.*
>
> *Frankly I think choice #3 is the easiest one to do."*
>
> —Luke Davis

match that is not very specific. They want someone whose goals and abilities are compatible with the mission of the company.

4. Ask Intelligent Questions. You took the trouble to prepare them. Don't pass up the chance to use them. With practice your confidence will grow, and you'll be able to pose thoughtful questions that occur to you during the course of the interview. Here are some possible questions to pose, but don't limit yourself to them. A healthy curiosity is probably your best guide.

Questions to Ask

1. Tell me about the kind of supervision I will get with your company.
2. Will I have any professional development opportunities?
3. Will I get to interact at all with upper management?
4. What projects will I be working on?
5. Will I do any traveling?
6. How likely is it for a co-op or intern to wind up working full-time with your company after graduation?
7. Will I have any opportunity to work in different divisions of your corporation?
8. Do I get to select which division of your corporation I work for?
9. How would you characterize the atmosphere of your workplace?
10. How would you characterize the typical employee at your office?
11. What most do you like about working for your organization?

■ After the Interview

1. Process the interview and determine next steps. Write it down while it's still fresh. Otherwise you might forget something important, or get different companies mixed up. Key bits of data are:

- **Recruiter's name and title** (double-check the spelling).
- **What you do next**—submit additional information? Contact them by a certain date? Make appropriate entries in your planner.
- **What they do next**—are there other stages to this company's selection process? Additional interviews? When will you hear from them?
- **Impressions of the interview**—good and bad points. This helps you prepare for the next interview.

2. Write a thank you note. This is more than being polite—it can close the deal. Use this letter to reiterate briefly why you match their needs. Did you forget to emphasize one of your strengths? Have you thought of any new reasons why you're the best qualified candidate for the position? Be sure to highlight that sort of information. One co-op student wrote:

> *I was so interested in the new project you mentioned that I tracked down an article on it in* Engineering Today. *I discovered that the laboratory equipment and processes being used are identical to what I will be using in my Chemistry class next semester.*

The thank you note can be just as powerful in the interviewing process as the cover letter. A strong one can reinforce the idea that you fit the employer's needs. A ho-hum one shows only that you follow business protocol.

■ Summary

Your objective during the interview is to demonstrate that you match the employer's needs.

Before the Interview

1. Conduct a thorough self-assessment (goals, experience, and skills).
2. Develop a good resume.
3. Research the company and industry.
4. Be familiar with typical questions and develop effective answers.
5. Dress appropriately.

During the Interview

1. Show enthusiasm.
2. Emphasize your selling points.
3. Sell yourself as a match.
4. Ask intelligent questions.

After the Interview

1. Process the interview and determine next steps.
2. Send a thank you letter.

CHAPTER 13
Teamwork

Why teamwork? Many students find group projects to be a nuisance at best and a disaster at worst. Things take longer when you work as a group. You don't have total control over the quality of the project. What about incompetents who pull the group's performance down? Or slackers who contribute nothing, but still expect the same grade that the other members earned? Isn't a camel a horse designed by a committee? Why teamwork, indeed?

The answer is that the benefits to teamwork outweigh the costs. Yes, working collaboratively with others poses special challenges, but effective teams get better results than individuals. The world of sports provides many examples of groups whose performance exceeds the sum of the individual players' abilities. On paper, Team A should dominate Team B, but they don't. Team B doesn't have the athletes or the individual skills to win, but they do. They win because they pull together, back each other up, and sacrifice for the good of the team.

Teamwork makes as much difference outside the sports world. As you will see in the chapter on leadership, teamwork helped Ford Motor Company become the most profitable American car manufacturer. Whether you plan to work in business or industry, education or medicine, the military or scientific research—teamwork makes a big difference. For this reason, people who recruit graduating seniors want to hire people who have demonstrated the ability to perform effectively in a team setting. In fact, a 1999 survey of 120 corporate recruiters conducted by Georgia Tech Career Services revealed that communication skills and teamwork were the two top qualities sought by employers. It should be apparent that the same corporations and organizations who prize teamwork in full-time employees will want team players to fill their co-op and internship positions. Moreover, your ability to function in a student organization, to live in a residence hall, and to get the most out of your college experience rests to a considerable degree upon your ability to work effectively with others in a group setting.

■ Signs of Effective Team Functioning

Parker observes in *Team Players and Teamwork* that "You get a certain feeling when you are part of a solid team. You enjoy being around the people, you look forward to all meetings, you learn new things, you laugh more, you find yourself putting the team's assignments ahead of other work, and you feel a real sense of progress and accomplishment." He elaborates by identifying twelve characteristics of effective teams:

1. **Clear Purpose**. Every member of the team knows the mission of the team and is committed to it.
2. **Informality**. There is typically a comfortable atmosphere, relatively free of tension or boredom.
3. **Participation**. All members contribute.
4. **Listening**. Members listen *actively* to what each other says. They attend to the meanings and feelings behind the words and demonstrate this by means of eye contact, verbal acknowledgement, mirroring, and asking encouraging questions.
5. **Civilized Disagreement**. It may surprise you to learn that good teams do not lack for conflict. The conflict is out in the open, however, and relatively free of personal attack. Moreover effective members work to resolve differences.
6. **Consensus Decisions**. Out of open, spirited discussion of differences emerges agreements that members can stand behind.
7. **Open Communication**. There are no hidden agendas because members feel free to express themselves candidly.
8. **Clear Roles and Work Assignments**. Members know their jobs and what is expected of them.
9. **Shared Leadership**. While there may be a titular leader, all members "own" the group and help facilitate the way the group functions.
10. **External Relations**. The group devotes some of its energies to maintaining useful contacts and resources outside of the group.
11. **Style Diversity**. There are a variety of types of team players represented. They perform different functions to promote team effectiveness.
12. **Team-Assessment**. The team is capable of examining itself, its processes, and how to improve its effectiveness.

It is very satisfying to work on a good team, but the purpose of the team is not to provide satisfaction. Nor is the purpose of the team to be a team. Effective teamwork is rather a necessary means to reaching an end. Katzenbach and Smith, in *The Wisdom of Teams*, are very clear on this point. The power of teams is exploited when the team is challenged to produce, when performance standards are high, and when the team and its members are held accountable for meeting those standards. Larson and LaFasto, in *TeamWork*, note that effective teams always have a goal that is both clear and elevating. Ineffective teams lose their focus on the goal. They worry more about power, who gets the credit, or what others will think.

■ Improving Team Skills

By developing team skills, you'll become a more effective student while in college. You'll also be investing in your future. If you can demonstrate that you're a team player, you'll be a more marketable job candidate. You will almost certainly be asked about your experience as a member of a team when you are interviewed for jobs as you approach graduation. And if you can play team ball on the job, you'll get better results leading to higher raises and more promotions. There are some obvious ways to operate when you find yourself in a task-oriented group—listen well, speak your mind, respect others' viewpoints, do your share of the work, help keep the group on task. It should be obvious that time and data management, important skills for individual success, are even more important for effective team performance.

Glenn has found that there are four roles within an effectively functioning team. Each role is necessary for a team to perform at maximum efficiency. While anyone can perform any of the four roles, you will probably gravitate toward the role most congruent with your own personality. As described in *Team Players and Teamwork*, here are the four roles:

- A **Contributor** is task oriented, provides solid technical information, does what is assigned, and insists on high standards.
- A **Collaborator** is highly goal-directed, is motivated by the mission of the team, is flexible, is receptive to new ideas. Sees the Big Picture.
- A **Communicator** is attentive to how the team is functioning, is a good listener, and encourages other members of the team.
- A **Challenger** questions goals, strategies, techniques, and ethics. Will confront authority. Willing to take risks.

While all roles are present in a strong team, any one of them can be counterproductive when taken to extremes. For example, the Challenger can intimidate others and demoralize the group if too critical or overly aggressive.

The roles within a team invariably support two separate, but equally crucial, functions: **person** and **task**. The person is any member of the team. Each member must be encouraged, supported, challenged, and heard. While every team member can support every other, typically some members are more adept at communication and encouragement. They listen actively and demonstrate their attention to the rest of the team by means of body language and eye contact. They nod their heads when others speak and mirror key words and phrases that capture a speaker's meaning. They ask others to elaborate on the point. They verbalize support and enthusiasm. They make sure that communication is open, disagreements are above board, and everyone contributes. The task is what the team is trying to accomplish—its very reason for being. For a team to be successful, it must stay on task. While every team member can be task oriented, there are usually some whose skills are especially strong in this area. They may have technical expertise or an especially clear picture of the mission. Their contribution is to keep the group on task, ensure that deadlines are met, and that the best methods and resources are used.

Every effective team is focused on its task. Every effective team supports and draws on each team member. Reflect on teams of which you've been a member. Who served these functions on the effective teams? How was one or the other function neglected on ineffective teams?

■ Stages of Team Development

Even as individuals develop over time, so do teams. In an important 1965 article, B.W. Tuckman identifies four developmental phases:

- ■ Forming
- ■ Storming
- ■ Norming
- ■ Performing

He compares group development to individual development. The first stage, **forming**, he likens to the dependency associated with infants and toddlers. Members are trying to figure out what the rules are and what the objective "really" is. Out of their confusion, they look to each other and the leader to try to make sense of their team and its mission.

The **storming** stage is likened to a rebellious child who fights parents and teachers. Hostility may occur and resistance to the task may be prevalent. If disagreements are suppressed, they may still emerge in covert ways: members not completing their tasks, the formation of factions, and straying from the task.

The **norming** phase is compared with an older child who begins to accept societal values and thinks beyond his or her own selfish wants. Informal rules are accepted and practiced. Commitments are made to accomplish the task around which the team is built. There is more open communication and cooperation.

The **performing** stage is likened to the healthy, productive functioning of a mature adult. Each team member is committed to the mission of the team and works collaboratively to accomplish that mission. Members work together by communicating openly and contributing willingly from their own resources.

■ So What?

What does all this have to do with you? Nothing—if you plan to be a hermit. If, however, you want to get the most out of college and enjoy a successful career, your mastery of team skills and understanding of group dynamics will be very useful. While you're in school you'll be expected to perform in groups, both within the classroom and as a member of campus organizations. In the workplace, outstanding team players are probably even more highly prized than they are on a college campus. Your ability to perform as a team player will mean greater opportunity, bigger raises, and more promotions.

■ Practical Steps in Working on a Team

Developing outstanding team skills can be a tall order because teamwork requires a collaborative spirit that doesn't come easily for everyone. Remember, however, that different personalities can contribute in different ways to team performance. You almost surely possess some characteristics which will help the teams of which you are a member. Here are some practical steps you can take to build on what you already have developed.

Habits to Cultivate

- Initiate discussions
- Solicit information and opinions
- Listen actively
- Express differences candidly
- Suggest techniques and strategies for fulfilling mission
- Clarify ideas
- Summarize
- Seek consensus
- Help team stay focused on task

Tactics for Running Effective Meetings

- Use an agenda and follow it
- Have a facilitator who promotes communication and keeps team on task
- Take minutes
- Draft next agenda
- Evaluate the meeting

■ Problem Areas

Dealing with Ineffective Members. Our students tell us this is one of the biggest challenges they confront as members of teams. Students may find their term grade is in jeopardy because some members aren't pulling their weight on a group project. While there are no foolproof remedies for this problem (If you invent a more foolproof system, someone will invent a bigger fool!), here are some things you can do to protect your grade and improve team performance.

1. Analyze the stage of group development. Your group may not have progressed past the forming and storming stages. Several members are inherently conscientious and quietly go about doing all the work. Group norms have not been established.
2. Confront the non-contributor. This is hard, but consider the alternative—more work for everyone else and maybe a poor grade. Speak to the other person(s) candidly, but diplomatically. Maintain eye contact, but don't glower. Don't attack the person, but rather state that the person's behavior is threatening everyone's grade.

3. Give the person a chance to explain what's going on. Maybe sickness or other obligations are factors.

4. Come up with a new understanding and a new deadline.

5. If all else fails, discuss your dilemma with your professor who may have some useful suggestions for solving the problem. Alternatively, many professors will not permit a slacker to ride the coat tails of more productive members. They may reorganize the team or take points off of the less productive member's grade.

Teamwork and Ethics. Chances are you'll be assigned to contribute to a group project before you graduate. You might not prefer the assignment. You might not like your team mates. No matter, you are ethically bound to contribute your fair share. Even as your grade is affected by the performance of others, so is theirs affected by yours. If you have special circumstances such as illness or a demanding work schedule, let the other members know right away. Try to find a way to do your part. It is neither professional nor honorable to accept a grade for work that you haven't done.

CHAPTER 14
Citizenship and Leadership

College prepares you to earn a living. Ideally, it also prepares you for life. Whether in the workplace or as a citizen, leadership will be an enormous asset. You will face challenges that you cannot meet by yourself. You will need the assistance of others. You will have to lead.

The modern workplace is highly competitive, and leadership is a highly prized skill. The people who recruit college graduates to work for their organizations are on the lookout for can-do, results-oriented candidates. As you approach graduation in a few years and start interviewing for full-time employment, you will almost surely be asked about your leadership experiences: Did you hold an office in any organization? Did you chair any committees? Tell me about a time when you served on a committee which was responsible for an important project, and the work wasn't getting done. What did you do to help the committee accomplish its mission?

For most of our history as a nation, college was an option for only an elite few. Those privileged to attend were expected to be leaders. This obligation to serve society transcended professional success. College graduates were supposed to be civic leaders as well. Society still needs citizen leaders—individuals whose commitment to the common good is expressed through thoughtful, informed action. Our nation—and the entire world—requires statesmen and women, informed voters, social activists, and philanthropists at every level.

The 21st Century will pose enormous challenges: environmental, violence, public health, and economic inequities to list but a few. Because technology has made the world small, other people's problems are now our own. If urban youth are alienated and unemployed, their rage threatens us all. If the Mexican economy flounders, we get more illegal immigrants. If the Russian economy fails, we are faced with the prospect of a new regime that may be hostile toward the USA. Local pollution becomes international acid rain. Global warming affects the climate and shoreline of all nations.

John Donne wrote that "No man is an island." Ernest Hemingway reminded us that the bell tolls for each of us. So, why should you regard it as your obligation to make your school, your city, your country, and your world a better place? Because we sink or swim together. Citizenship is for the common good. Citizenship is also in your own interest.

Let us add that this is not an ideological position. It transcends liberal and conservative perspectives. Indeed this is one of the few principles upon which all our national leaders agree even though they may be divided as to just how to address the enormous challenges facing us. Conservative thinker William F. Buckley extolled the concept of voluntary national service in his recent book, *Gratitude: Reflections On What We Owe to Our Country*. President Clinton implemented a national service corps. So, whose job is it to be a better citizen? Yours and ours.

■ Leadership

In order to make a better world, we need better leaders. Citizenship requires leadership. So does professional success. If you can lead no one, your education is incomplete. True, you probably won't be President of the United States, a Four Star General, or the CEO of a major corporation. (But then, why not?) More likely, you will be a director, a teacher, or an entrepreneur. And you will almost certainly at some point chair a committee, head a project, propose an idea to neighbors or colleagues, or parent a child. Each and every one of these roles/activities requires you to lead. How do you do it, and can you learn the skills it takes?

The Components of Leadership

We believe there are at least six characteristics that make for successful leadership:

- Vision: a sense of the future and its possibilities.
- Ethics and integrity: a commitment to think carefully about the public good and our own values when we act.
- Service orientation: the habit of working for others.

- Communication skills: the ability to say and write what we mean, simply and powerfully as well as the ability and commitment to listen with understanding to the concerns of others.
- Self awareness: the ongoing realization of personal strengths and weaknesses, of knowledge of interests, values, temperament, aspirations, and abilities.
- Teamwork in diverse groups: skills to accomplish common goals by working with others who bring a variety of experiences to the task.

Let's take a brief look at each.

VISION. Before you can lead someone to the promised land, you must be able to see it yourself—even if you haven't been there yet. Indeed, the greatest leaders are able to create the future by vividly imagining it. John Kennedy envisioned a man on the moon. Stephen Jobs envisioned a world in which we all use personal computers. Mary Kay envisioned a network of small business women who were also saleswomen creating a business juggernaut. Why couldn't your vision be greater still?

While we encourage you to dream big, we also know that not every business prospers, nor is every dream realized. Nor is every vision about changing the world. Sometimes it's about changing a small part of it—seeing the successful child in the troubled youth you mentor, seeing a team that wins by playing together, picturing a residence hall in which students are a community of learners.

A vision is related to the goals that together will make the vision a reality, but a vision isn't a goal or even a collection of goals. A vision is a portrait of a future you wish to create. Although it comes from your imagination, it is something you can describe vividly. It is something that you can see and so you can describe it to others. A vision can sustain you in tough times. It can compel others to work together in the service of that vision. It can unite, motivate, and provide a common direction.

Where do visions come from? How do you become visionary? We believe you can become more visionary, but like everything else, you acquire vision only by paying your dues. First, you must understand yourself. You must know YOUR values, interests, abilities, and goals. You must create YOUR mission before you can create one that others will buy into. Second, you must know the world around you. You cannot create a new world (or even a small part of it) without first understanding the present one. You need to know the field or domain in which you would lead. You will also be well served to know something of the world beyond that field. True innovation often emerges from the synthesis of disparate ideas from seemingly unrelated fields. Ignorant, uninformed people are not likely to develop very useful, much less compelling visions.

Leaders face almost constant new challenges. They must come up with new strategies and techniques for coping with a world undergoing revolutionary change. While leaders must be grounded in solid, enduring values they must keep abreast of technical, scientific, and cultural changes. How can any business compete if it uses outdated information technology? How can medicine advance apart from genetic research? How can marketing executives sell new products if they don't know the mood of the public? Ted Turner, owner of a regional television station in Atlanta, read Alvin Toffler's *Future Shock* and envisioned an innovative way of communicating the news around the world. Eventually, his vision matured into a media empire revolving around CNN. In 1998, Turner was named man of the year by *Time Magazine.*

Probably the most important characteristic you can possess is an insatiable curiosity—a burning desire to learn. This desire must translate into action—reading, experimentation, involvement, reflection. You would be short-sighted to confuse going to college with acquiring an education. You would be a fool to pass up the education that's available to you while you're here. Moreover, right now is the time to cultivate the successful habits of the continuous, life-long learner. If you are not making quantum leaps in knowledge acquisition from here on out, you will be shortchanging yourself in the vision department and therefore in the domain of leadership.

Finally, the most compelling organizational visions resonate with constituents because the constituents had a role in developing the vision. Sometimes, this occurs indirectly because a leader knows her followers so well that she is able to incorporate their values and aspirations into a vision that resonates with the rank and file of the entire membership. On other occasions, leaders explicitly ask for input from members? What shall our strategy be? What should our organization look like a year from now?

ETHICS AND INTEGRITY. Before individuals will follow someone's lead, they must believe in that person. Leaders, therefore, must be true to their words. Their walk must match their talk. James Kouzes and Barry Posner, two of the most influential scholars of leadership today, argue that a leader's credibility with constituents is the absolute "sine qua non" of leadership. Why commit yourself to a cause to which the leader claims to be invested, but who behaves otherwise?

Ethics are important because leaders exert power. That power can be expended for good or evil. A dictator, such as Adolf Hitler, had many qualities that made him a powerful leader. He was able to mobilize large numbers of people to commit to a common cause. The cause to which he enlisted the German people, however, was based upon ethnocentrism. He led his people toward ignoble ends. His leadership caused death and suffering almost beyond imagining. While membership in the human race carries with it the responsibility to behave honorably, leaders must bear an even heavier responsibility. When they pursue the common good, society is enriched. When they do not, others will suffer.

Ethics are important because without them organizations cannot flourish. Customers do not want to buy from a company they don't trust. Customers won't come back to a store that sells faulty products. Organizations perceived to be unethical may not last very long. Members of an organization will form a culture that is based upon the practices of its leadership. If managers, directors, vice-presidents, and CEO's lie to their employees and fail to keep their promises, the employees soon start lying to management. As deceit and petty politics rise, morale and productivity plummet. This is true whether the organization is a giant multinational corporation, a local high school, or a college fraternity.

There is inevitably an ethical component to leadership. Think of great leaders, and you think of honorable men and women. This doesn't mean our greatest leaders were saints, but they are remembered as having a firm moral center. It's not enough to have good ideas and charisma. You must have a coherent set of values. Your actions must match your words. If people don't know where you stand, they will not want to back you. If people doubt your word, why in the world would they want to follow you?

SERVICE ORIENTATION. We usually think of charismatic leaders by virtue of their ability to deliver stirring public speeches. While inspirational speech-making is a useful leadership skill, research conducted by Jay Conger and Rabindra Kanungo reveals that constituents will commit to a leader's cause only when the leader is perceived as serving organizational ideals rather than merely self interest. Moreover, those leaders were regarded as more charismatic when they were perceived as serving the organization and its members.

Robert Greenleaf's name is synonymous with "servant leadership." He was profoundly influenced by reading Herman Hesse's *Journey to the East* in which the leader of the journey is initially mistaken by his fellow travelers as a "mere servant." Eventually, the travelers come to realize that this humble servant is the glue that holds the group together, maintains their safety, and keeps them headed in the right direction.

You can intimidate some people into following your lead, but people follow out of fear only so long as you have some power over them. Most of us do not typically have that

sort of positional power over those whom we would influence. If you want to be an effective leader of a student organization, you will be effective because you are somehow able to connect with members who volunteer their time and energy. Even in the business world, the best managers and executives know that their best staff members are, in essence, volunteers. Top employees can always get good jobs somewhere else.

The best leaders motivate people to *want* to follow them. How do you get people to want to? Communicating a compelling vision certainly helps, but others won't even consider your vision unless they're convinced you have their well-being at heart. Think about some leader whom you would gladly follow through thick or thin.

Chances are, you believe this person respects you, cares about you, desires your success. The best leaders exude concern for their colleagues and constituents.

You demonstrate concern for those whom you would lead by being considerate, by understanding them, and by encouraging them. While your first image of a leader might be some take-charge person giving an inspiring speech, you must learn to listen if you want others to listen to you. Good leaders are empathic: they can see things from the other person's perspective. The very best leaders understand others deeply, grasping what events mean to their followers. Because good leaders know their followers well, they know what resources are needed in order for the followers to complete their missions. Much of a good leader's energy is devoted to preserving the well-being and morale of every member of the organization and of securing the resources to enable members to do their jobs. A true leader, then, serves the organization and its members.

Servant leaders, then, are committed to their followers and to their organization's ideals. Ideas are cheap. Let us amend that. Ideas—even good ones—without the commitment and dedication to turn them into action are cheap. Many a lofty vision has died because the person who dreamed it did not invest the blood, sweat, and tears to make that vision a reality.

Think back on when someone wanted you to work for a cause. Did the captain ask you to sacrifice for the good of the team, but (s)he never passed the ball? Didn't make you very committed to the team, did it? Did the president of your organization ask you to work Saturday morning at the fund raiser, but (s)he slept in? Maybe next time you'll sleep in too. Leaders who aren't committed to serving their organization and its members soon have no one to lead.

Commitment starts in the heart. It is feeling passionately about something. Commitment, however, always boils down to action. It is standing up for your ideas. It is working long and hard without complaining to turn ideas into reality. So, how do you get committed? How do you kindle passion in your heart for something beyond yourself? How do you become a servant leader?

If nothing fires you up, we suspect you're avoiding life rather than living it. If you are a young adult just out of high school, you probably enjoy more freedom in your life than you have ever had or ever will have. You can spend your time playing computer games, watching TV, and taking naps. Or you can immerse yourself in academic and extracurricular life. You can join a professional society, start a small business, or work for Habitat for Humanity.

Sometimes, motivation fires you up to take action, but if nothing motivates you, we urge you to act anyway. Once you start thinking, doing, and serving, enthusiasm will follow. In a recent discussion on leadership a number of fraternity and sorority officers revealed to me (Bill) what they thought most held their organizations back. Too many of the members didn't want to get involved, didn't want to assume responsibility for improving things, didn't want to stick their necks out. They were waiting for the other members to fix things. The following story, created by the prolific Anonymous, neatly captures this problem.

"Four people named Everybody, Somebody, Anybody, and Nobody met to accomplish an important task. Everybody was sure Somebody would do it. Anybody could have done it, but Nobody did it. Somebody got angry about that, because after all, wasn't it Everybody's job? Everybody thought that Anybody could do it, but Nobody realized that Everybody wouldn't do it. It ended up that Everybody blamed Somebody when Nobody did what Anybody could have done."

COMMUNICATION SKILLS. OK, you have a great idea—an idea that is positively visionary. It's almost certain that you will need help to make your vision a reality. How do you get others to buy into your vision? Throughout this book we've emphasized the importance of communication skills. In order to lead you must communicate your vision to the people whom you want to help you. Not only must you paint a clear picture, you must persuade others to make a commitment to work with you towards the realization of your vision.

This is partly a "public speaking" issue. Can you stand up in front of a group and speak confidently and sincerely? Can you do this before a handful, a dozen, a roomful, a thousand? Speaking effectively before a group may intimidate or even terrify you, but it is a VERY useful skill. Among the activities that most executives claim to like is speaking before large groups.

This doesn't mean that you have to be a declaimer of olympian proportions in order to be a leader. Some people are more persuasive one to one. If you saw the movie, *Malcolm X*, you may recall the lengthy conversations Malcolm had with the inmate instrumental in his conversion. The other inmate rarely raised his voice. Nor were his words flowery. But he spoke from the heart and convinced Malcolm to work for a much larger cause than himself.

In the business world, would be leaders are encouraged to master the art of the "parking lot speech." Everybody is busy, and the only time you have to sell your idea to a colleague may be in the minute or so when you meet in the parking lot on the way to or from the office. For students, the analog is the "walk to class speech." You run into somebody whose support you need, and you have just minutes together on your way to History class. Can you boil down your ideas so they are clear and simple, yet still persuasive before you reach the classroom?

If you are not sure of your persuasive abilities, work to improve them. Consider some of the following ways to improve this essential skill:

- Take a class in public speaking
- Attend an assertiveness workshop
- Participate in a sales seminars or workshop
- Volunteer to give a committee's report to the group-at-large
- Join an organization such as Toastmasters
- Run for office in an organization
- Try out for a part in a play

The written word is also an important tool for those who would lead. George Washington had Thomas Paine's words disseminated to every member of his army. These words helped to create a common understanding of why the revolutionary soldiers were fighting and increased their commitment to that cause. An executive with experience in both the public and private realm recently underscored to me the importance of writing clearly. Almost every day in the workaday world, you must write reports, memos, letters, summaries, and proposals. Your success hinges partly on how well you write. Moreover, if you write poorly, you leave a tainted track record. The only knowledge of your work that the CEO possesses might be your proposal. If it's laced with grammatical errors, misspelled words, and awkward phrasing, it is unlikely that your proposal will find favor. It is even less likely that your star will rise in the organization.

Communication is, of course, a two-way street. You must receive information from others as well as dispense it. Listening with sensitivity for the deeper meanings and emotions behind the words of others is vital for leaders. As one saying goes: humans have one mouth and two ears. This is nature's way of reminding us that we should spend twice as much time listening as speaking. Listening is crucial for leaders for a variety of reasons. Through active listening, a leader can learn about the concerns of the members of an organization. By listening attentively, a leader demonstrates concern for those members and thereby motivates them. By listening, a leader can get ideas which will influence the very direction an organization takes.

SELF AWARENESS. As a leader, your biggest resource is yourself. Does it not, therefore, make sense to know as much as possible about this resource—strengths and weaknesses, beliefs and values, skills and abilities. If you understand your weakness in public speaking, you can work on improving that skill. You can also delegate that responsibility to another member of your team who will better express your organization's perspective. I once had a very bright assistant who was blind to his inability to communicate in plain English to an unsophisticated audience. On several occasions, he mistakenly assumed he had persuaded his audience to buy his ideas when the only thing he had convinced them of was that he couldn't speak simply and clearly.

In Chapter 2 of this book, we urged you to cultivate a clearer self-understanding while you were in college. If self awareness is valuable for every person who would be educated, it is crucial for those who would lead. In Chapter 2, we suggested that psychological tests were one useful means of self-exploration. In fact, it is routine for individuals entering management training and leadership development programs to be given a battery of tests. Extensive feedback is provided to the trainee by a skilled clinician. Further feedback is provided by other trainees and trainers to corroborate the testing. It is commonplace for employees in many organizations to receive 360 degree feedback—feedback from bosses, colleagues, subordinates, and even customers. The purpose of all this feedback: to promote self-awareness.

Warren Bennis, in *On Becoming a Leader*, states that to "know thyself" is to understand clearly the differences between the way you define yourself and the way others define you. Leaders create change. Since not everyone likes change, those who interact with leaders may define them quite differently than would the leaders themselves. Some will assume a woman lacks the toughness to lead. Others will assume that a person of color possesses insufficient talent for leadership. There are countless ways that constituents can dismiss someone's leadership—too new to the organization, the wrong age, from the wrong part of the world, from the wrong social class. It is the leader's firm sense of self that will enable that person to perform in the face of such resistance.

It is not just that leaders know themselves, however; it is that they constantly try to improve themselves. Leaders use their self awareness as a springboard for recreating themselves. When they discover deficiencies, they work to overcome them. They read, they train, they study successful leaders, they seek out the experiences which will enable them to grow.

TEAMWORK IN DIVERSE GROUPS. Think back for a moment on some of your experiences as a member of a sports team, a member of a committee, or one of a team charged with completing a project. It is highly likely that you can recall some team member who was domineering, self-absorbed, inattentive, unfocused, argumentative, or irresponsible. Remember how frustrated you felt, how disheartening it was to have to cope with this character. You could have won the game, but Chris let everybody down because of poor practice habits. You could have had an outstanding organization which consistently got first-rate results, but Pat held the entire organization back because of a giant ego. Perhaps the group was able to compensate for the counter-productive member, but it made it harder for everyone else.

Managers and corporate recruiters are quite aware of the importance of teamwork. Business and management writers have covered many organizational success stories that were powered by effective teams. Katzenbach and Smith, in *The Wisdom of Teams*, cite a number of examples: Motorola was able to design and manufacture the world's leading cell phone. Ford became the most profitable American automobile company through teamwork. Teams are critical to 3M's ongoing success. The Desert Storm military victory over Iraq could not have been accomplished without the extraordinary teamwork it took to move 300,000 men, 100,000 vehicles, and 7,000,000 tons of equipment, fuel, and supplies. In Harlem, the first Little League in forty years was introduced through the efforts of a group of citizens working together. Glenn Parker surveyed fifty-one companies and reports in *Team Players and Teamwork* that effective teamwork consistently resulted in greater productivity, more effective use of resources, and better problem solving.

Student organizations are no different. Fraternities and sororities, sports clubs, and professional societies are less successful without teamwork. No officer wants to take on new members who impede group progress. Therefore, you must be a team player in order to succeed in today's world. Team skills are crucial for your professional success. They are also necessary for your success as a student and as a developing leader.

In *The Breakthrough Team Player*, Andrew DuBrin lists skills and attitudes that make for effective teamwork including:

- Assuming resonsibility for problems
- Willingness to commit to team goals
- Ability to see the big picture
- Belief in consensus
- Willingness to ask tough questions
- Helping team members do their jobs better
- Lending a hand during peak workloads
- Rarely turning down a co-worker request
- Openness to new ideas
- Recognizing the interests and achievements of others
- Active listening and information sharing
- Giving helpful criticism
- Receptiveness to helpful criticism
- Being a team player even when personally inconvenienced

In other words, the more fully human you are, the better a team player you will be, and the better a leader you will be. Needless to say, this is an ongoing life-long process of learning and development.

Not only must you collaborate, you will be called upon to collaborate effectively with people who are very different from yourself. In fact, much of the power of teamwork comes from combining the contributions of diverse talents and perspectives. The increasing complexity of today's business world requires such "alchemy." Better decisions are generally made by groups of diverse people. Moreover, in a global economy, you will be expected to work with people from all over the world.

Think of an outstanding football team. It is comprised of many talented athletes pulling together for a common cause. Perhaps the star is the quarterback. However talented that quarterback, the team would not be as effective if it were comprised of eleven outstanding quarterbacks. None would have the weight or strength to play on the line. They would probably not have the speed to play tailback, receiver, or in the defensive secondary. A successful sports team requires not just talent, but different kinds of talent. The same is true of a corporation. Scientists and engineers must be able to work together with accountants, managers, marketing specialists, and advertisers.

Most of us are more comfortable working with people like ourselves. Engineers like working with engineers and writers prefer the company of other literary types. Once you enter the workforce, however, you will be expected to collaborate with people whose skills and outlooks differ from your own. If accountants called all the shots, the company might never take any risks. If engineers called all the shots, aesthetics and design might suffer. If artists ruled, the new widgit might triumph aesthetically, but sink financially.

You must also be able to work with people whose race, religion, politics, and lifestyles are unfamiliar or, at any rate, different from your own. The American workforce of the future will be diverse. If you can't work with differences, your career will suffer.

■ Learning to Lead

We believe that learning to lead is imperative for every college student. Yet many students are notoriously indifferent to the leadership opportunities available to them. Leadership certainly requires careful reflection. Taking classes, attending speeches, and reading books about leadership can provide students with both insight and inspiration about their own capacity to lead. We believe, however, that leadership is a "contact sport." You learn by entering the fray. If you are not a member of an organization, if you never vote, if you avoid participating in the governance of your residence hall—your commitment to learning to lead is questionable.

In order to get a college degree, you are required to take an array of courses, including core course, courses in a major, and a smattering of electives. Chances are, you are NOT required to study leadership either in the classroom or through your involvement in campus activities. You will be cheating yourself, however, and jeopardizing your career if you do not resolve to improve as a leader. Today's apathetic student is tomorrow's indifferent citizen whose very inactivity amounts to fiddling while society burns.

While we urge you to cultivate your capacity to lead, do not make the error of confusing a position or an office with true leadership. While chairing a committee, presiding over an organization, and joining campus organizations all provide excellent leadership developmental opportunities, none of these inevitably guarantees excellence. That comes from practicing the six habits we identified at the top of this chapter. Leadership then is about serving others and operating ethically. It is about envisioning how to make things better and communicating that vision effectively. Leadership is about understanding yourself and collaborating with all kinds of people. These are six skills which are as important as anything you will ever learn, and no matter how committed you are to cultivating them, you will never master them. Like most things in life that matter, learning to lead is a life-long process. It's time to get started!

■ Leadership Self Assessment

Vision

In order to be "visionary," you must first be well-informed. Today, that means being a continuous learner, both in school and on your own. How many of the following statements can you affirm?

_____ 1. I frequently read a daily newspaper.

_____ 2. I can name four political columnists of varying ideological points of view.

_____ 3. I frequently read a weekly news magazine.

_____ 4. I often watch a national news show on television.

_____ 5. I often read a business periodical (e.g., *Wall Street Journal, Fortune, Business Week,* etc.)

_____ 6. I follow the latest developments in science and technology.

_____ 7. I've been to a play within the past year.

_____ 8. I've seen a movie with subtitles within the past year.

_____ 9. I have read an unassigned work of literature within the past year.

_____ 10. I periodically read a professional or trade journal within my field of interest.

_____ 11. I attend meetings or conferences of a professional society.

_____ 12. I've learned some new computer skills within the past year.

_____ 13. I sometimes discuss my field of interest with others to find out more about it.

_____ 14. I have attended a serious concert/performance within the past year.

_____ 15. I occasionally watch television documentaries that cover history, science or current affairs.

_____ 16. I have eaten the food of at least six different countries within the past year.

_____ 17. I have friends and acquaintances of a variety of ethnic and religious backgrounds.

_____ 18. I can readily identify most countries on a world globe.

_____ 19. I understand some basic features of most major cultural groups throughout the world.

_____ 20. I have read a serious nonfiction book which was not assigned within the past year.

_____ 21. I know the basic tenets of each of the world's major religions.

What other actions do you take to indicate your commitment to continuous learning?

What do your responses reveal about your commitment to continuous learning? What do you need to do differently in the future?

■ Ethics and Integrity

Name an individual whom you judge to be high in integrity: _____

How long have you known this individual? _____

_____

How long did it take before you recognized the person's integrity?

_____

_____

What characterizes this person that spells integrity?

_____

_____

What actions does this person take that suggest integrity?

_____

_____

Can you identify a situation in which this person's integrity was tested?

_____

_____

How did (s)he handle the test?

_____

_____

Name an individual whom you judge to lack integrity: _____

How long have you known this individual? _____

How long did it take before you recognized the person lacked integrity?

_____

_____

What characterizes this person that spells weak integrity?

_____

_____

What actions does this person take that suggest weak integrity?

_____

_____

Can you identify a situation in which this person's integrity was tested?

_____

_____

How did (s)he handle the test?

_____

_____

In what related ways are you like the person with high integrity?

_____

_____

In what related ways are you like the person with weak integrity?

_____

_____

How will you increase your personal integrity?

_____

_____

■ Service Orientation

There are many ways you can serve others: through the political process, through philanthropic work, and through your demeanor in daily interactions. Check those items below which reflect YOUR personal behavior:

_____ 1. I'm registered to vote.

_____ 2. I vote in most elections.

_____ 3. I know who my congressman is.

_____ 4. I've worked in a political campaign.

_____ 5. I know the news well enough to be an informed voter.

_____ 6. I contribute money in support of my beliefs.

_____ 7. I contribute time in support of my beliefs.

_____ 8. I stay informed of the causes I'm committed to addressing.

_____ 9. I contribute money to the cause.

_____ 10. I contribute time and energy to the cause.

_____ 11. I'm a member of a group which serves the cause.

_____ 12. I avoid activities which harm the cause.

_____ 13. I compliment people when they succeed.

_____ 14. I congratulate people when they win an award.

_____ 15. I encourage people when they have setbacks.

_____ 16. I send notes or e-mail to encourage people.

_____ 17. I keep track of people's birthdays.

_____ 18. I send birthday cards to friends and acquaintances.

_____ 19. I give gifts or stage a surprise when a colleague achieves something big.

_____ 20. I work more for organizational goals than for personal glory.

Communication

_____ 1. I can be silent when others need to speak.

_____ 2. I can hear the feelings and meanings behind the words.

_____ 3. I can ask questions that encourage self-revelation.

_____ 4. I avoid criticizing other persons.

_____ 5. I convey my interest by eye contact and body language.

_____ 6. I ask questions in class.

_____ 7. I contribute to class discussions.

_____ 8. I offer my views during meetings.

_____ 9. If I disagree strongly during a meeting, I'll say so.

_____ 10. I can effectively report a committee's discussion back to the main group.

_____ 11. I can run a meeting effectively.

_____ 12. I know Robert's Rules of Order.

_____ 13. I can address a small group effectively.

_____ 14. I can hold a large group's attention when I speak.

_____ 15. I can make a strong case for my point of view.

If you're not satisfied with your persuasive skills, here are ten antidotes.

1. Prepare a meaningful question before class. Ask it during class.

2. Prepare a thoughtful observation before class. State it when appropriate during class.

3. Think about an issue likely to come up at your next meeting. Ask for the floor, and make your point.

4. Think about a perspective with which you're likely to disagree at the next meeting. Prepare a rejoinder. State your rejoinder at the next meeting.

5. Volunteer to speak for your committee.

6. Volunteer to run a committee meeting. Prepare an agenda, and stick to it.

7. Study Robert's Rules of Order.

8. Volunteer to speak before a small group on something that's important to you. Prepare thoroughly, and practice your speech.

9. Volunteer to speak before a large group on something that's important to you. Prepare thoroughly, and practice your speech.

10. Try to convince a friend or acquaintance to join you in some cause.

Self Awareness

It is difficult to assess yourself accurately. For example, answer the following question: Are you blind to your own faults? Even if you are, your blindness prevents you from knowing it. There are some habits that suggest an openness to self-examination that are worthy of cultivating, however. How many do you practice?

_____ 1. I read any critique of my work made by a professor and reflect on it.

_____ 2. I attempt to understand my personality survey scores in this class.

_____ 3. I solicit feedback from others about my performance.

_____ 4. I am willing to take some moderate risks in order to improve as a leader.

_____ 5. When others criticize me, I honestly try to weigh the validity of their remarks.

_____ 6. I compare my own skills to those discussed in this chapter.

_____ 7. When I read other leadership literature, I use the ideas to look at myself.

_____ 8. I can honestly identify some areas in which I need to improve myself.

_____ 9. I can honestly identify some areas of personal strength.

_____ 10. I use experiential activities in class and workshops to learn about myself.

Teamwork

_____ 1. I contribute my fair share on group projects.

_____ 2. When I disagree with other team members, I say so.

_____ 3. When forming a team, I try to select diverse talents.

_____ 4. I understand the stages of group development.

_____ 5. I understand how my personality best contributes to team performance.

Putting It All Together

Most of us will never head up a major corporation or hold a major political office. Nonetheless, we can exert leadership in many ways—by holding an office in a smaller organization, by speaking up at organizational meetings, by volunteering to handle a problem. Here are some ways you could stretch your leadership wings.

1. Identify an issue about which you have strong, unexpressed feelings in an organization to which you belong. Think about what you could say or do to strengthen the organization's stand on this issue. Craft a statement which you could make at a meeting. Imagine what it would be like to make the statement. What would the response of your fellow members be? Can you think of effective ways of responding to them? Pick an ally within the organization that you could share your views with. How does (s)he respond? Does (s)he have any suggestions for improvements? Are you accurately understanding the opposing point of view? Select a time when you will raise the issue and state your position. Go for it!

2. Identify a concern or a problem which you have. Then identify a person in authority who could address your concern. Think of a *reasonable* course of action which the authority could take to improve the situation. Make *sure* that the authority has the power to effect the change you recommend, that the action is cost-effective, that it will not cause undue damage elsewhere. Craft a recommendation you could make to the authority. Practice it with an ally. Make an appointment with the authority. When you meet, explain your concern, recommend your solution, and state your willingness to help implement the solution, if that's feasible.

3. Identify an office or position you would like to hold. It should be in an organization in whose goals you believe. Declare your intention to run for office. Or, if more appropriate, speak with current officers about your desire to assume a greater leadership role. If you run for office, secure the commitment of some friends who will help you. Get organized, plan a campaign, implement it. If the more likely route to power is through appointment, discuss your desire to serve on a particular committee or as a particular office holder. Explain why you think you can do the job. Ask for feedback and a commitment to be given the opportunity to lead.

4. Read some books and articles on leadership and citizenship.

5. Attend a leadership workshop.

6. Sign up for an academic class in leadership.